Written with pastoral warmth, a [...] a solemn awareness of the eternal [...] the tragic story of Judas Iscariot ca[...] [...]pressing disciples not to give up on the Lord Jesus, as Judas did.

Jonathan Prime
Director of Pastoral Ministries and Director of the
Fellowship of Independent Evangelical Churches

My favorite part of knowing pastor Colin is how blessed I've been through his teaching! From the beauty of the Thief on the Cross to the ultimate betrayal, Pastor Colin stays true to the scriptures as he takes us on a journey, using his authentic and often poetic gift of storytelling to once again provide us with a unique and powerful perspective on the life of Judas.

Stephen Baldwin
Actor

Colin Smith's earthy and compelling story of Jesus through the eyes of Judas will encourage you to never give up on the faith. And if you have 'turned back and abandoned the faith I once professed,' the words of Judas may be painfully familiar. But it is not too late to turn back. Smith gives hope for recovery of the things that really matter in life and relationships. And he answers the deep questions about identity, friendship, being famous, and having things our own way. All in the mouth of Judas, the one who eternally regretted giving up Jesus.

Ed Stetzer
Billy Graham Distinguished Chair, Wheaton College, Illinois

Of all human beings, none passed so close to the gates of heaven on his way to hell than Judas Iscariot. His story, expertly told here by Colin Smith, is an urgent cautionary tale for each one of us.

Tim Challies
Founding blogger of Challies.com
Pastor at Grace Fellowship Church in Toronto,
and author of several books

'Prone to wander', as an old hymn expresses it, is a recurring problem in the life of faith. Here's a superb antidote, expressed through the tongue of an unexpected source, Judas Iscariot. Creative, insightful and deeply, deeply challenging, *Heaven: so near, so far* is a page-turning must read. Highly recommended.

Steve Brady
Principal of Moorlands College,
Christchurch, Dorset

HEAVEN, SO NEAR - SO FAR

THE STORY OF JUDAS ISCARIOT

COLIN S. SMITH

CHRISTIAN
FOCUS

UNLOCKINGTHEBIBLE.ORG

Colin S. Smith is Senior Pastor of The Orchard Evangelical Free Church in the northwest suburbs of Chicago. His preaching ministry is shared through the daily radio program, *Unlocking the Bible* and through his website, UnlockingtheBible.org.

paperback ISBN 978-1-5271-0091-6
epub ISBN 978-1-5271-0133-3
Mobi ISBN 978-1-5271-0134-0

Published in 2017 and reprinted in 2018
by
Christian Focus Publications Ltd.,
Geanies House, Fearn, Ross-shire,
IV20 1TW, Scotland, U.K.
www.christianfocus.com

Cover design by Daniel van Straaten
Printed in the U.S.A.

CONTENTS

As many go to heaven by the gates of hell
so more go to hell by the gates of heaven

MATTHEW MEAD

A Note to the Reader

I wrote this book because I want you to see that Jesus Christ is of supreme value, and that following Him is worth any cost.

My prayer is that, whatever your failures, disappointments, or unanswered questions, you will come to a place of saying, 'I cannot and will not give up on Jesus Christ.'

Peter, who denied Jesus, and Judas, who betrayed Him, both hit a low point in their lives when it looked as if they were done with Jesus forever. Yet these men responded in very different ways. Judas separated from the other disciples and gave up on faith in Christ completely. Peter chose a different and a better path. Though he had denied the Lord, he rejoined the other disciples. Christ restored Peter and gave him a new purpose in life for which he was empowered by the Holy Spirit. And the fruit of Peter's restored life was incalculable.

The tragedy of Judas is that he could have received the same grace and restoration as Peter. Christ forgives the sin of all who come to Him. But rather than returning to Jesus, Judas gave up on Him.

Friend, if you are struggling with the faith you once professed, or if you are hanging on but feel you lack the strength to continue, I pray that your future path will be like Peter's and not like Judas'. Christ rose. The tomb is empty. And that means that the future belongs to Him.

COLIN S. SMITH

Introduction

I came as close to heaven as a person can be, without getting in. For three years, I followed Jesus Christ and devoted myself to ministry. I was in the boat when Jesus calmed the storm. I served the bread and fish when He fed five thousand people. As an apostle, I was sent out to preach the gospel, I cast out demons, and I called people to repentance. But today, despite all that I did as a follower of Jesus, I am languishing in hell.

Down here, we are all familiar with the story of the thief on the cross, to whom Jesus said:

'Today, you will be with me in Paradise.' He was on the brink of hell, but ended up in heaven. My story is different. I was at the gates of heaven, but ended up in hell. I was the disciple who betrayed Jesus.

I want you to know that I was neither a helpless victim nor a hideous monster. I was a person with hopes, dreams, doubts, fears, disappointments, and frustrations very much like you. When I abandoned my faith, I felt that I had good reasons for doing so, though now, I live with perpetual regret.

In telling my story, I seek neither your pity nor your praise. I write only to describe the path by which I came to this abyss, having spent the best years of my life as a disciple of Jesus.

1

Ambition

From my earliest days, I wanted people to know who I was. Thousands of people live and die without being celebrated or remembered. I hated that. I didn't want to be one of them.

Like most boys, I looked up to my father. He was a kind, gentle man who worked hard as a shepherd and managed to provide a modest, but happy home for our family. From what I could tell, people around our town thought my father was a decent man, but I don't ever recall anyone speaking highly of him or what he had accomplished. He was, in a word, uninspiring.

There were, however, two men in our town who captured my imagination. One was a highly successful farmer who found a way to bring the best fresh fruits I had ever seen back to our area for sale. Most families in our town grew olives, but these could hardly compare to the figs, pomegranates, and apricots this man was offering. While other merchants barely scraped by, this man cleaned up. Suffice it to say, this farmer was talked about by everyone we knew, as were the many possessions his success enabled him to acquire.

The other man I admired was a distinguished physician who was rumored to have trained in Egypt. In those days, doctors were closely tied to the synagogues, working to cure the sick alongside the priests, whose role was to pronounce them healed. There was a certain swagger about this man that I enjoyed, and most of the people in our town looked at him with a sense of awe. The idea of following in his footsteps as a physician never occurred to me, but I vividly remember wanting people to show me the same admiration and respect that they showed him.

Plain and simple, from my earliest days, I was ambitious. I wanted to make a name for myself. Yet, apart from an aptitude for numbers and an uncanny ability to calculate loans, debts, interest, and repayments, I did not possess any extraordinary gifts or talents. Intuitively, I realized that I needed to attach myself to something or someone. I needed to find a cause that would propel me, a movement that would be the making of me.

I thought I had found it when, at the age of twenty-nine, I first heard rumors about an eccentric prophet who was preaching up a storm in the desert. I was curious about him, and so I decided to go and see for myself.

The man was dressed in camel's hair, and he sustained himself for long stretches in the desert on a diet of locusts and honey. His message was simple: 'Something that has never happened before in human history is about to take place: The Lord is coming! You are going to meet with God! Make straight the way of the Lord.'

People who heard him realized that if they were going to meet with God, they had better do some confessing and repenting first, and John the Baptist had a way in which they could respond to his message: a baptism of repentance for the forgiveness of sins.

John touched a chord with his message and the crowds grew exponentially as people from Jerusalem and Judea, where I had grown up, came to hear him.

John's preaching was powerful. When he said, 'The kingdom of heaven is at hand,' I felt as if God Himself might open the heavens and appear at any moment. People who heard him lined up to confess their sins and to be baptized, and such was the impact of John's ministry that a delegation of priests and Levites were sent from Jerusalem to find out what was going on.

'Who are you?' they asked? To which John answered: 'I am not the Christ.'

That surprised me. The 'Christ' was the long-promised Messiah whose coming would bring the blessing of God and usher in His kingdom. Feeling the power of John's preaching, and seeing the response of such vast crowds to his message, it had occurred to me, and no doubt to many others, that John might indeed be the Messiah.

But John was emphatic about this: 'I am not the Christ, and I am not worthy to untie the strap of his sandal.'

Now my interest was really engaged. I had thought that John might be someone I could follow, but he was pointing to someone else. Whoever this person was, I wanted to meet Him.

It was when I was with the crowds in the desert that I caught my first glimpse of Jesus. John was preaching as on any other day, when he saw someone coming toward him and said: 'Behold, the Lamb of God, who takes away the sin of the world!'

Having been taught the Old Testament Scriptures, I knew well the story of Abraham telling his son Isaac that God would provide a lamb, and how the animal that was provided took the place of Isaac on the altar.

I had been brought up on the story of the Exodus, in which our ancestors painted the blood of a lamb over the doorways of their houses. God had said: 'When I see the blood, I will pass over you.'

So when John identified Jesus as the Lamb of God, he was saying that Jesus would be the substitute who would die in the place of others, and that He would be the sacrifice whose blood would be shed for the protection of His people.

This I understood, but it was what John said next that really got my attention: 'This is he who baptizes with the Holy Spirit.' Growing up, I had been fascinated by the stories of the judges; men like Gideon and Samson who accomplished extraordinary things when the power of the Holy Spirit came upon them. But the Scriptures spoke repeatedly about how, in the last days, God would pour out His Spirit in a new and greater way. If that was going to happen, I wanted to be part of it.

Putting the pieces together, I knew that I was onto something big. John said that God's reign and rule on earth was at hand. He had called people to prepare themselves by getting ready for the coming of the Lord. Now, he was pointing to Jesus and announcing that He had the ability to drench others in the power of the Holy Spirit. If even a small part of this was true, the opportunity would be enormous. I felt sure that my moment had come.

I was not the only one who felt this way. The first to follow Jesus were Andrew and John. They became disciples through the preaching ministry of John the Baptist. Andrew then brought his brother Simon to Jesus, who gave him the name Peter.

Philip's story was different. As far as I could tell, he was neither directed to Jesus by a preacher nor introduced to Jesus by a friend. Jesus found him, stepped into his life, laid hold of his heart, and called him to become a disciple.

These four men had one thing in common: they were all from Bethsaida, a small fishing village on the shore of the Sea of Galilee. This made it clear to me that, although Jesus was known to be from Nazareth, Galilee would be the base of His operation. The time had come for me to pack my bags, leave my home in Judea, and try to stake my claim for a place in His inner circle.

By the time I arrived in Galilee, the ministry of Jesus had already begun. Taking up where

John had left off, Jesus declared: 'The king-dom of God is at hand; repent and believe in the gospel.'

In these early days, the first disciples were sometimes with Jesus, but at other times, they returned to their work on the boats. With the circle around Jesus still evolving, I wanted Him to see me as the reliable one, the one on whom He could depend, so I made it my business to show up wherever Jesus went.

As Jesus moved from town to town, His pattern was to teach in the local synagogue. I would arrive early and sit where He would see me. And sure enough, it worked. When He looked at me, He gave me that knowing look that said, 'So you are here again! I'm glad about that!'

At first the crowds around Jesus were quite small, but as word about Him spread, that soon changed, and things really started to take off after the Sabbath He spent in Capernaum. As soon as He began to speak that morning, a man possessed by an evil spirit shouted out: 'What have you to do with us, Jesus of Nazareth? Have you come to destroy us? I know who you are— the Holy One of God.'

Jesus rebuked the man: 'Be silent,' He said, and then, 'Come out of him!'

The man fell to the floor in a convulsion, and the evil spirit came out of him with a shriek.

The thing that was so striking to me in this was the authority of Jesus. The demon knew who He was, and fled at His command.

After the service, Jesus went to the home of Simon Peter and Andrew. Peter's mother-in-law had taken ill with a fever, but when Jesus took her hand, the fever left. Word about this spread, and by evening, people from all over the town had arrived with loved ones who were sick or oppressed by evil spirits. Many were healed that night and, of course, that led to even larger crowds the following morning.

As the crowd grew, people became restless. Peter came to the door and told us that Jesus was not in the house, but assured us that He would be there soon. Later, Andrew came out and said the same thing, though he was clearly less certain. As the morning wore on, it was evident that nobody knew where Jesus was; a full-scale search was under way. We waited all day, but He never showed up. Eventually, the people went home disappointed, and I remember thinking to myself, *This is the sort of thing He needs to avoid. If I get into His inner circle, I will do something about it.*

A few days later, Jesus was back in Capernaum again, performing a miracle so spectacular that His reputation in the town was completely restored. When word got around that He was back, a crowd even larger than the ones we had seen before gathered in and around the house where Jesus was staying.

As usual, I had arrived early and was sitting close to Jesus as He taught. By this time He knew me by name, and I could count on a knowing smile from Him. That small gesture was huge for me. It made me feel that I might be someone on whom Jesus would choose to depend.

Teaching is never easy with the distraction of a large and restless crowd, but on this occasion, the chaos reached another level. While Jesus was speaking, I became aware of some noise above us, and guessed that some people had clambered up onto the roof. How many were there I wondered, and how long would the roof hold up?

Some dirt began to fall from the ceiling, and then more, until a hole opened, and, looking up, I could see four men who had dug through the roof with their hands. Then, to the astonishment of everyone in the room, they lowered a paralyzed man, lying on his bed, delivering him right in front of Jesus.

Now that's ingenuity, I thought. *Here are people who are committed, determined, and resolved: people who know what they want, and will do whatever it takes to overcome all that stands in their way.*

The words Jesus spoke to the man on his bed were not what I had expected. 'Son,' He said, 'your sins are forgiven.'

Why did He say that? I wondered. Forgiveness of sins is important, but it did not seem to be the man's most obvious need. It seemed as if, to Jesus, being forgiven by God mattered more than the ability to stand up and walk!

I don't think I was the only one who questioned this. People all around the room became unsettled. They looked at Jesus as if to say, 'Is that it? What about the fact that this man can't walk?' Others were offended that Jesus had pronounced the man's sins forgiven. Sins, by definition, are offenses committed against God, and God alone has the right and the authority to forgive them.

Jesus must have known this. He told the people that He wanted them to know that He had the authority to forgive sins, and for that reason, He said to the paralyzed man: 'Rise, pick up your bed, and go home.'

When the man did what Jesus said, the whole crowd was amazed, and I remember thinking, *Never in my entire life have I seen anything even close to this.*

After this, a growing crowd followed Jesus everywhere He went. As news of what happened in Bethsaida and Capernaum spread across the country, people came from Jerusalem in the south and even from Tyre and Sidon in the north to see for themselves what was going on.

Whoever Jesus was, His ministry was taking off, and, knowing that John had attracted huge crowds in the desert with his plain call to repentance, I figured there was no limit to what Jesus could do, propelled by His miraculous power.

I was ambitious. I had no interest in attaching myself to an obscure cause destined to failure. But I felt that, in Jesus, I had found a winner, and I became more determined than ever to find my way into His inner circle.

With the crowds following Jesus growing by the day, and so much competition for His attention, it was clear to me that something would have to be done to establish a fixed circle of people who would give themselves full time to traveling with Jesus and supporting Him in His ministry. With all my heart, I wanted to be one of them.

One day, we got word that after a whole night alone on a hillside praying to His Father, Jesus was ready to choose the disciples who would share most intimately in His life and ministry.

Word soon spread among His friends, and all of us made our way to join Him on the mountain. He told us that He would appoint twelve, and that their calling would be first, to be with Him, second, to preach, and third, to cast out demons. Knowing that a life-shaping moment had come, we were all silent as we waited to see who He had chosen.

Looking at the crowd in front of Him, Jesus began calling out names:

'Simon Peter and Andrew,' He said, prompting the brothers who were first to follow Jesus to step forward from the crowd.

'James and John,' He continued, selecting the brothers He referred to as 'Sons of Thunder'.

'Philip and Bartholomew.' So far, no surprises. Bartholomew I had first known as Nathaniel, and he, like the others, had been with Jesus from the beginning.

Six of the twelve had been chosen. Six more spots remained.

'Matthew!' Now that was a surprise. Matthew was a tax collector, which meant that he had sold out to the Romans, lining his pockets at the expense of his own people. Hardly a popular choice. Nor, as I saw it, a wise one. Why would Jesus trust Himself to a man who had broken faith with his own people? Matthew was, to my mind, the kind of man who could easily turn out to be a traitor.

'Thomas!' Another strange choice, I thought. This man had followed Jesus faithfully, but he also asked a lot of questions. There was a certain hesitation about him, and I wondered if he would ever be able to overcome his many doubts.

'James, the son of Alpheus!' I had never heard of him, and frankly was never sure why he was chosen.

'Simon the Zealot!' Now that was a risky choice. Simon was known as the Zealot because of his involvement in radical politics. Seeing him stand with the other nine, I wondered how it would be possible for Simon and Matthew to get along, given their histories on opposite sides of the political divide.

Only two spots remained, and the tension of waiting was becoming unbearable. Then He called out my name: 'Judas!' But He wasn't looking at me. He was beckoning Thaddaeus, who brought all kinds of confusion because he was known by three names, Judas, Thaddaeus, and Lebbaeus.

One spot left: *God, please let it be me!*

Jesus paused, and then, looking directly at me with intensity and compassion in His eyes said, 'Judas Iscariot!'

I was in!

2

Mission

By any standard, we were a strange group. There were two of us named Simon (Simon Peter and Simon the Zealot), two of us called James (James the brother of John and James the son of Alpheus), and two of us known as Judas (Judas the son of James, and me, Judas Iscariot).

The name 'Iscariot' refers to Kerioth, the town in Judea where I was born and raised. The name stuck, perhaps to distinguish me from the other Judas, who suffered the indignity of being described as 'Judas (not Iscariot)'. Nobody remembers him. I was the one who would be known throughout history.

Being in the inner circle gave me a unique insight into Jesus. From the earliest days, it was clear to me that He was pursuing two strategies at the same time. The first was to reach the mass of people, bringing hope through His miracles and wisdom through His teaching. The second, and arguably the more important, was to train His inner circle. This was a shrewd decision and, without it, what transpired in His name would never have taken place. His approach to training was simple: He brought us with Him to watch, took us aside to learn, and sent us out to do.

With regard to watching, I had already seen remarkable things before being appointed as an apostle. But they were just a prelude to the wonders I witnessed in the years that followed.

I will never forget the day Jesus attracted one of our largest crowds. The plan for that day had been for us to take a few days' retreat with Jesus, and so we got on the boat to head for a quiet and secluded place. But some people saw us leaving and, guessing where we were going, made their way around the shore, gathering others as they went. By the time we arrived at what was supposed to be a desolate place, a large crowd had gathered.

Another crowd of people was the last thing we needed, but Jesus had compassion on them. To Him, they were like sheep without a shepherd, so He taught them, giving Himself to them as if He had all the time in the world and nothing else to do.

Having looked forward to a quiet retreat, I found the intrusion of this crowd exasperating, and I was not alone. We wanted some time with Jesus for ourselves, but we all felt that since these people had made the effort to come, the right thing would be to give them some teaching and then send them home.

But that was not Jesus' way. Hour after hour passed, and when Jesus showed no sign of drawing things to a close, we became increasingly agitated. Late in the day, we decided that we had no option but to intervene.

We pointed out to Jesus the rather obvious facts that we were in a remote place and that the day was almost gone. We pressed on Jesus that something would have to be done, and that our preferred option was that He should dismiss the crowd while there was still time for them to buy food on their way home. There was no way we were going to be able to feed everyone, and the last thing we needed was a hungry and demanding crowd on our hands.

Jesus responded by telling us to give them something to eat, which of course was impossible.

Then, He asked Philip, 'Where can we buy bread so that these people can eat?' Philip, to his great credit, pointed out that a basic meal for 5,000 people would cost the best part of a year's wages. I knew that we did not have that kind of money, and so it was clear to me that we were not in a position to give these people a meal. Besides, where would we buy it?

But Jesus was resolute. He had told us to give the people something to eat, and having established that we did not have the money to buy food, He directed us to find out how many of the people had brought food with them. 'How many loaves do you have?' He asked. 'Go and see.'

The results were not encouraging. Andrew took the lead on this, and all he found was a young boy with fives loaves of bread and two fish. He brought the boy to Jesus simply to make the point that, having done the research, it was clear to him that next to nothing was available.

What happened next amazed everyone who saw it. Jesus told us to have the people sit down in groups of fifty or 100. When they were settled, Jesus took the loaves and the fish from the boy, looked up to heaven, gave thanks, and then began breaking them. The best way I can describe the next few moments is to say that the loaves and fish multiplied in His hands. What He broke, He gave to us, and yet when He gave, He still had more in His hands ready to be broken.

It occurred to me that Jesus could have invited the people to come and receive this food directly from His hands, but this was not His plan. He had told us to give the people something to eat, and, having led us to the conclusion that this was completely beyond our ability, He now gave us the means to fulfill His own command.

As Jesus multiplied the bread and the fish, He gave the food to us, and we had the honor of taking it to the people. I received from Jesus as much bread and fish as I could carry in my arms and took it to a group of a hundred people who were watching in amazement. When my arms were empty, I came back to Jesus, and received another armload of food from Him. The other apostles did the same. Together, we were runners for Jesus, receiving from Him in order to give to others. When we came to Him, our hands were empty. When we left Him, our hands were full. Meeting the needs of the people made me feel like I was walking on air. With power like this, anything was possible.

Most of our days were less dramatic. Jesus often taught us through stories, or parables as He called them, that, once heard, left a lasting impression.

One of these was His story about a farmer who scattered good seed on different kinds of soil. The point of the story, as Jesus explained it, was that we should not be surprised when our efforts in ministry brought disappointing results. Seed falling on the path gets snatched away. Seed sown among thorns get choked, and seed in shallow soil soon withers. But seed that falls on good ground will produce a good crop that could be as much as thirty, sixty, or even 100 times what was sown. The story reminded us that we should persevere in the ministry of sowing the Word, even at times when we were discouraged by immediate results. We should do this in the conviction that the long-term outcome of this work would be a great harvest.

But there was another side to His teaching that always struck me as strange. In His story about the sower, He seemed to suggest that the ground in which the seed was sown represented different kinds of people. If that was the case, there would be some people on whom the ministry of Jesus would have no effect. There would be others in whom His message would produce an immediate and enthusiastic response, but it would only last while things went well with them, and, in the face of trouble, their first instinct would be to abandon the faith they had professed. And there would be others again who, having professed faith in Jesus, would be lured away by the deceptive power of money and a desire for other things.

I found this hard to imagine. Listening to the end of Jesus' story, where He described the abundant harvest, I said to Thomas, 'That's me! I want to see a hundred-fold return on all that I am investing in this enterprise!'

Speaking of the strange things that Jesus said, one that stuck in my mind was when he told us: 'Not everyone who says to me, "Lord, Lord," will enter the kingdom of heaven.' He seemed to suggest that some who had spoken truth in His name and others who had driven out demons in His name might, in the end, not enter the heaven they had proclaimed to others.

The idea that someone blessed with the power to cast out demons in the name of Jesus would not be known by Him made no sense to me. But since Jesus knew the twelve of us by name, I assumed that these disturbing words could not apply to any of us. It was really hard for me to imagine how anyone could be involved in ministry, and not be known by Jesus, but these words stayed with me: 'Not everyone who says to me, "Lord, Lord" will enter the kingdom of heaven, but the one who does the will of my Father who is in heaven.' Bad news for some, but since we were clearly doing God's work, and doing it with Jesus Himself, I figured I was good.

As we traveled, we watched and listened to Jesus with an eager sense of purpose. From the beginning, He made it clear that He was training us for ministry, and part of that training was to send us on a mission.

Jesus told us that He was giving us authority over demons and power to cure sickness, and that He was sending us out to proclaim the kingdom of God. None of us had ever preached before, but, having listened first to John the Baptist and then to the preaching of Jesus, I felt that I was ready to give it a try.

The scope of our mission was limited to the area immediately around Galilee. Our approach was simple: when I arrived in a village, I made it known that I was an apostle of Jesus, which immediately created interest. Word about Jesus had spread widely, and coming in His name guaranteed us an audience.

We traveled light, believing that God would supply our needs through people who believed our message. In most places, I found people who were willing to open their home to me, which was good, because Jesus had sent us out without money. 'You received without paying; give without pay,' He had said. *Reasonable for a short trip like this,* I remember thinking, *but hardly a practical policy for the long term.*

Once my presence in a village was known, people brought the sick to me, just as they had brought the sick to Jesus. I anointed them with oil, and, to my great joy and delight, saw many of them healed. Then there were people so possessed by the power of evil that they were unable to resist the compulsive behaviors to which these powers drove them. When they came for help, I commanded these evil spirits to depart, and again, to my joy, they left. I followed this up by calling people to repent, much as John the Baptist had done, and with similar results.

The whole experience of that mission trip was exhilarating, and when we gathered to give our reports to Jesus, I found that the others had felt the same. God had been at work, and He had been working through us! We had been given power, and this power seemed to open endless possibilities.

News of our mission spread, even reaching the ears of Herod the Tetrarch. He could hardly have been counted among our supporters, but the fact that our work had gained the attention of the king was another sign to me that I had made the right decision in following Jesus. Not only was His fame spreading, but now our work as His apostles was becoming known, to the point that even Herod saw our movement as a force to be reckoned with.

All of us were in high spirits. We felt that all things were possible. But despite the power of His miracles, the wisdom of His teaching, and the success of our mission, there were some things about Jesus that caused me concern and, over time, made me increasingly uncomfortable.

3

Frustration

It often bothered me that, when the twelve apostles were listed, I was always the last to be named. But I took some comfort from something Jesus said about the last being first and the first being last. If that turned out to be true, it would be bad news for Peter and good news for me.

Given my position at the end of the line, I was always looking out for ways to advance my cause, and, given my ability with numbers, it seemed natural that I should offer to serve as treasurer for our ministry.

Accounting is not glamorous work, but I knew its importance. Holding the purse strings would give me a certain power over the others, and I saw this role as an opportunity not to be missed.

There were thirteen of us on the road, and from time to time others joined us, expanding our group and increasing our costs. None of us was paid, but we all had to eat, and, as treasurer, I saw it as my responsibility to make sure that we would never run out of funds.

I was always looking to attract the kind of people who could help bring our ministry to a broader audience. However, to my growing frustration, Jesus had a habit of letting our best opportunities slip away.

The first time it happened was when a highly successful entrepreneur came asking for help. I could see that he was serious from the way that he knelt before Jesus. I could also see that he was loaded.

'Good teacher,' he said, 'What must I do to inherit eternal life?'

My pulse quickened. Here was a man who clearly had the means to fund our entire operation. I was already counting on his money as if it were in the bag. Before Jesus answered his question, my mind was racing to what this man could do for us if he got on board. *If Jesus plays this right,* I thought, *we will be funded for life!*

The man's objective was to inherit eternal life, and from the way he framed his question, it seemed clear that he was ready to do whatever it would take.

Jesus started out by pointing the man to the commandments: 'Do not murder; do not commit adultery; do not steal; do not bear false witness; honor your father and mother.'

The man seemed pleased. 'I've been doing all these things since I was a boy,' he said.

Then Jesus said, 'You lack one thing…'

This was the moment. I held my breath, waiting for Jesus to tell him that life could be his if he would join us. And that is exactly what Jesus did say: 'Come, follow me.' But He blew it, both for the man and for us, in what He said first: 'Go, sell all that you have and give to the poor.'

There were two problems with this. First, it was asking too much. The sensible approach would have been to draw the man into our circle and then ask him for more as our relationship deepened. But no! With Jesus, it was always the same: All or nothing! He insisted on reigning as the supreme Lord over all who professed to follow Him, and I could see that, with the resources this man had, what Jesus was asking would be impossible.

The second problem was that giving to the poor was the wrong use of the money. What good would this man be to our group if he off-loaded all of his assets before he joined?

The man's response was predictable. His face fell. He got up from his knees and walked away from Jesus. Having come with great antici-pation, he left with great sadness.

Looking at this from my position as treasurer, I could only see it as a wasted opportunity. This man was the kind of person who could really make things happen, and if only Jesus had said: 'Come, follow me, and you can help us with our mission,' the man would have joined us gladly.

That encounter left a bad taste for all of us, and it led Jesus to take us aside for a candid con-versation on this issue of money: 'How difficult it is for those who have wealth to enter the kingdom of God,' He said.

We were all amazed. Surely not! But Jesus was insistent: 'It is easier for a camel to go through the eye of a needle than for a rich person to enter the kingdom of God.' To me, this seemed ridiculous. If those who made a success of their lives could not get into God's kingdom, who in the world could?

Jesus looked at us directly, as He always did when He came to the point He most wanted us to remember. 'With man it is impossible,' He said, 'But not with God. For all things are possible with God.'

Looking back on Jesus' conversation with the entrepreneur in the light of what He told us afterward, I can see, at least in some degree, what Jesus was getting at.

The man was all about himself. 'What can *I* do to inherit eternal life?' 'All these commands *I* have kept since I was a boy.' It was all about what he had done for God. But the message of Jesus was not that a man could have eternal life through what he could do for God but through what God could do for him.

The man was confident that he had kept the fifth, sixth, seventh, eighth and ninth commandments. But when Jesus called him to sell all that he had and give to the poor, He exposed the fact that the man had not kept the first commandment, where God says: 'You shall have no other gods before me!'

I wonder if he got that? Did he come to see that Jesus was leading him away from his illusion of being a law-keeper, and confronting him with the reality that he was a law-breaker who needed to cast himself on the mercy of God? I never found out, and I don't suppose I ever will.

Money often came up in the teaching of Jesus. I had always thought of money as a friend, but Jesus taught us that money has power. He spoke about money as a master, as if it were a rival god seeking to make you its servant and to take control of your life. 'No man can serve two masters,' Jesus said. 'For either he will hate the one and love the other, or he will be devoted to one and despise the other. You cannot serve God and money.'

Money is like fire: a good friend and a terrible enemy. Kept in its place, it has the power to sustain you, but when it takes control, it has the power to destroy you. Believe me: I know. Money became my master, and it wants to become yours. It is a power, and unless that power is brought into submission, it will run and rule your life.

Another opportunity came to us in Jericho, a town that we passed through as Jesus, against all of our advice, made His way toward Jerusalem.

We met a man in that town who was seriously rich and genuinely interested in getting to know Jesus. His name was Zacchaeus.

Matthew, who I had come to know well since we had been traveling together, had made good money as a tax collector. But Zacchaeus was a *chief* tax collector, and that put him into the top league when it came to earnings.

Crowds lined the streets as we arrived in Jericho and, though I did not see the man hidden in the branches of a tree, Jesus did. He addressed him by name: 'Zacchaeus, hurry and come down, for I must stay at your house today.' Zacchaeus was delighted, and warmly welcomed us into his home.

Jesus' decision to seek hospitality in the home of Zacchaeus did not go down well with the crowd. Tax collectors were notorious for their corruption. Offering themselves as servants of the Roman occupation, they were despised by their own people as traitors.

One motive moved them to walk on this shameful path: Money! A small extra charge added to the tax levied by the Romans and then creamed off the top by the tax collectors added up, over time, to some serious money! And Zacchaeus ran this racket for the entire city.

To the people of Jericho, Zacchaeus was the worst of the worst, and they could not understand why Jesus would seek out one of the town's most notorious sinners. But I had a different view. To me, Zacchaeus represented another opportunity to recruit someone who could resource our ministry and expand our sphere of influence. 'If this man joins us,' I said to Matthew, 'We have it made.'

I did not hear what Jesus said to Zacchaeus, but I did hear his response. He said that he would give half of all that he had to the poor and that he would return any money he had taken by fraud, four times over.

Jesus rejoiced. 'Today, salvation has come to this house,' He said.

I was fuming. I barely managed to hide my irritation. If Jesus had asked Zacchaeus to give half of his money to us, he would have done it gladly. Instead, we left—rejoicing in the blessing of God that had come to Zacchaeus, glad for those who would receive generous compensation for what had been taken from them, but having gained nothing for the funding of our ministry.

To be the treasurer under such circumstances, where opportunities to bring in game-changing gifts were so carelessly squandered, was always disheartening, often exasperating, and sometimes downright infuriating.

It wasn't just the opportunities to raise money that were wasted. Often when our crowds were growing, Jesus would speak in a way that was obscure or sometimes even offensive. People who might easily have been drawn in were alienated and left us instead.

The worst example of this happened at what I thought was our supreme moment of opportunity: that astonishing occasion when Jesus fed over 5,000 people by multiplying the loaves and the fish. The crowd was so impressed with what they saw that they were ready to make Jesus king right there in the desert.

It was clear to me that the time had come for us to ride the wave of their support and take our movement to the next level. But Jesus had no interest in their attempt to politicize His mission, and, instead of seizing the moment, He slipped away from the crowd.

The following day, when word got around that we were back in Capernaum, many who had been fed in the desert arrived, looking for more. The words Jesus spoke to them were hard to understand. 'I am the bread of life,' He said. 'Whoever comes to me shall not hunger and whoever believes in me shall never thirst.' Then He accused them of not believing, which surprised me, first, because they had made the effort to come and hear Him, and second, because even if true, such a direct approach was hardly the way to win their favor.

Not surprisingly, the crowd became restless, but Jesus just kept going.

'No one can come to me unless the Father who sent me draws him,' He said. Well, that was hardly a message that would win friends and influence people!

But then it got worse. Jesus said: 'Whoever feeds on my flesh and drinks my blood has eternal life. For my flesh is true food, and my blood is true drink.'

People found this offensive. But Jesus insisted that the reason they found it hard to hear was that, although they all professed to be His disciples, some of them did not believe.

It was as if Jesus was sifting the crowd, intentionally sorting out those who had really submitted to His authority from those who had merely been caught up in the crowd of His followers. Well, if Jesus was trying to lose His crowd, He certainly was successful. Many who at one time had been with us turned back, and Jesus just let them go.

I was devastated. For so long, we had been working to build a mass movement. We had been blessed with great success, and now, in a single day, so many people who had joined us were gone.

The twelve of us looked at each other in stunned silence. How could Jesus lose so many people? Then He asked us, 'Do you want to go away as well?'

Peter spoke up first: 'Lord, to whom shall we go?' he asked. 'You have the words of eternal life, and we have believed and have come to know that you are the Holy One of God.' It was a ringing endorsement and affirmation of Jesus, but I was not sure if Peter was speaking for all of us. What was Thomas thinking, I wondered?

Then Jesus said something quite extraordinary: 'Did I not choose you, the twelve? And yet one of you is a devil.'

At the time, this made no sense to me at all. How could one of *us* be a devil? We were Jesus' disciples. We had left everything to follow Him. We were the ones who had been *casting out* demons! What could the devil have to do with any of us?

At no time had Jesus said anything remotely like this before. But now, He was making it clear that He had known from the beginning that someone would betray Him. He did not say who this would be, but He made it clear that one of us in the inner circle had thoughts of desertion and was capable even of treachery. Despite all my doubts and frustrations, it never occurred to me that I might be the one.

4

Objection

The last straw for me came during a dinner served in honor of Jesus at the home of a man called Simon who, at one time, had suffered from leprosy. Simon had been healed by Jesus, and, having been delivered from the miserable existence of an outcast, he opened his home for a gathering of friends to celebrate all that Jesus had done.

In truth, I would rather not have been there in the first place. Our past visits to Jerusalem had been marred by threats of violence, and the twelve of us were of one mind that we should avoid the capital and its surrounding districts at all costs.

Trouble had flared up in Jerusalem when Jesus again offended a crowd He might easily have won. He had been speaking to people who believed in Him about how the truth would set them free. They took offense at this, reckoning that, as descendants of Abraham, they were free already.

Jesus then told them: 'If anyone keeps my word, he will never see death.' Rather than causing them to rejoice, this made them really mad. They pointed out that since Abraham had died, Jesus must be claiming to be greater than Abraham, to which Jesus said: 'Before Abraham was, I am.' This was too much for them, and they picked up stones to throw at Him, but Jesus slipped away, as He had done on other occasions.

The same thing happened some time later, when we were in Jerusalem for the Feast of Dedication. As usual, a crowd gathered around Jesus, asking Him to tell them plainly if He was indeed the Messiah.

Jesus said that He had already told them. Their problem was not that He had been unclear but that they did not believe. As if this were not enough, He went on to tell them that the reason they did not believe was that they were not among the sheep given to Him by His Father.

Then Jesus said something that, to their ears, sounded like blasphemy: 'I and the Father are one.' When Jesus said this, the crowd again picked up stones with the intent of putting Him to death.

Seeing that the mood was turning ugly, the authorities tried to arrest Jesus, but again He slipped away, and we all escaped across the Jordan to a quieter and more peaceful environment, where many people welcomed Jesus and His message.

It was while we were there that Jesus received word that one of His closest friends had become ill. The friend's name was Lazarus, and the cry for help was sent out by his sisters, Martha and Mary. I knew that Jesus loved these friends dearly, so I was surprised when, on hearing the news that Lazarus was sick, Jesus seemed to pay no attention.

I was also relieved by His inaction. Bethany, where Lazarus and his sisters lived, was just two miles from Jerusalem, and, after experiencing the hostility of the temple crowds, I knew it would be a mistake to go there again.

But two days later, Jesus announced that we were going to Bethany.

We all looked at each other in shock. Thomas spoke up for the rest of us: 'Rabbi, the Jews were just now seeking to stone you. Are you really going there again?'

Going so close to Jerusalem at a time when there was such intense hostility toward Jesus seemed like inviting trouble. But Jesus was resolute, and then He told us why: 'Lazarus has died' He said.

There was nothing any of us could do. Jesus was going, and our only decision was whether we would go with Him. I felt sure that if we went, we would be putting our heads in the jaws of a lion.

By the time we arrived at Bethany, Lazarus had been in the tomb for four days. The mourning, of course, continued, and there were many who had come to comfort Martha and Mary in their loss.

Martha came out to meet us, 'Lord,' she said to Jesus, 'if you had been here, my brother would not have died.' Jesus assured her that her brother would rise again. Martha agreed. She had always believed what the Scriptures say about a day of resurrection at the end of time. But Jesus said to her: 'I am the resurrection and the life. Whoever believes in me, though he die, yet shall he live.'

When Mary came out to meet Jesus, she fell down weeping at His feet. Jesus was deeply moved, and began to weep Himself. Then He asked about the tomb.

Lazarus had been buried in a cave with a stone set in front of it. Jesus told the mourners to take away the stone. Before we knew it, the stone had been removed and Jesus was shouting in a loud and commanding voice: 'Lazarus, come out!' To my complete amazement, Lazarus came out, walking in the linen cloths in which he had been wrapped for burial.

This miracle exceeded anything else that Jesus had ever done. It was stunning in itself, and staggering in its implications. If Jesus could raid the realm of the dead and call people out at will, nothing would be impossible for Him.

So, we had plenty to celebrate when we gathered at Simon's house with Martha, Mary, and Lazarus. Simon had been quarantined, but now he was our joyful host. Lazarus had been in the grave, but now he was reclining next to Jesus, engaged in animated conversation with his friends.

Looking around the room, I noticed Mary's eyes moving from Jesus to her brother and from her brother back to Jesus. Having gone through the agony of losing Lazarus, she had experienced the love and comfort of Jesus, standing with her in her sorrow, and then she had witnessed a glorious demonstration of Christ's power in which her brother had been restored to life and given back to her.

It was not surprising to me that Mary wanted to express her love and gratitude to Jesus. But what she did next brought me to a moment of clarity that would propel me onto a new and deadly path.

At one point in the evening, Mary brought out a large flask of perfume. My eyes widened as I recognized its value, the equivalent of an entire year's wages. I had no idea that we had an asset like this in our group, and if Mary was ready to give it up, it was the kind of gift that would really make a difference.

Mary approached Jesus and, opening the bottle, began pouring the perfume over His head. I had no problem with Mary anointing the head of Jesus with this perfume as a sign of her devotion. The problem was that she kept pouring. The perfume was about a pint in volume, and, as Mary poured it out, it ran over Jesus' shoulders, soaked into His robe, and, eventually, dripped down onto His feet. When the last drop had been poured from the bottle, Mary knelt before Jesus, and wiped His feet with her hair.

What a waste! The extravagance of this left me cold. It seemed like fanaticism to me. And a complete misuse of a valuable asset. Something needed to be said. I needed to express my strong objection, and so as Mary moved away from the feet of Jesus, I motioned to her and took her aside.

'What in the world do you think you are doing? Do you have any idea how much that perfume was worth? It would take me a year to earn enough money to buy that, and in a single, reckless moment, you have just blown the whole lot!

Mary was ready with her reply. 'Judas,' she said, 'you don't know much about love. To you, the cost of the perfume made what I did wrong. To me, the cost of the perfume made what I did right.'

I was not the only one who thought that Mary's act of devotion was excessive. Several of the others spoke up in support of me, saying that what Mary had done was a waste. They were right, and I had nothing but contempt for what she had done.

The trouble with taking a stand is that you expose yourself as the target, and sure enough, John went after me as I had gone after Mary. In my frustration over what she had done, I took the moral high ground, and asked, 'Why was this ointment not sold, and the money given to the poor?'

Looking back, I don't know why I brought the needs of the poor into the conversation. If I had been responsible for the money that could have been gained from the sale of the perfume, I certainly would not have given it to the poor. That would be as wasteful as pouring the perfume over Jesus.

But John used this against me. 'Judas, you are not saying this because you care about the poor!' he said. 'You are saying this because you are a thief. We trusted you with our common purse, and you have been helping yourself to the money. The reason you want the perfume sold is so that you can get your hands on it.'

It was an outrageous accusation, and I knew he had no proof. I'll admit that from time to time I would borrow from the bag, but it was always with the intent of returning what I had taken.

Then Jesus came to Mary's defense. 'Leave her alone,' He said, 'She has done a beautiful thing to me.' Then, looking directly at me, Jesus said: 'You always have the poor with you, but you will not always have me.'

There was no doubting the rebuke. Jesus had been clear in His teaching about giving to the poor, and He did not contradict what I had said about its importance. His point was that I had failed to discern the unique significance of the moment in which we all found ourselves. 'She has anointed my body beforehand for burial,' He said.

When Jesus spoke about His burial, the mood among the disciples changed. At first, they had agreed with me in my outrage at the waste, but now they repositioned themselves in the light of Jesus' words. The moment of tension passed, and the celebration resumed. But not for me. I looked on at the joy of the others as if I were watching through a window from the outside.

It was clear to me that there had been a profound change since the sunny days when the twelve of us committed ourselves to Jesus. I had seen great potential in the crowds we had drawn, an extraordinary resource in the ability of Jesus to perform miracles at will, and a unique opportunity in the ministry we had built. But ever since we set out on that long journey to Jerusalem, Jesus seemed to be absorbed in contemplating something quite different. He spoke about giving His life as a ransom for many. He repeatedly said that the Son of Man must be killed, and told us that if we wanted to follow Him, each of us must be ready to take up a cross of his own.

This gloomy talk did not appeal to me, and the more I heard it, the more uncomfortable I became. If Jesus wanted to lay down His life, that was for Him, but I had no interest in laying down mine. I was interested in building a future. I had followed Jesus with this in view, but after three years, our ministry seemed increasingly like a tale of missed opportunities.

When we attracted crowds, Jesus spoke words that were hard to receive and people wandered away. When we engaged the interest of friends who could move our ragged outfit to the next level, Jesus let them go. The rich entrepreneur, the chief tax collector, the crowds who wanted to make him king—all gone! And now this waste of the perfume! There seemed to be no end to it.

Even now, as I think of it, the memory of that waste gets to me. A whole year's wages! I still think the right move would have been for Mary to give the perfume to me so that I could sell it and invest the money. But no! Here we were with yet another chance to build some equity for the group, yet the opportunity slipped right through our fingers.

Three years had passed since I joined up with Jesus, and what had come of it? Jesus repeatedly failed to make the pragmatic moves on which the building of any mass movement depends. The result, which I as treasurer saw only too plainly, was that after three years our shared purse was no greater than it had been at the beginning.

Beyond that, it was clear to me that the tide was turning against Jesus. The raising of Lazarus may have been Jesus' greatest work, but it was also the trigger that brought hostility toward Him to an entirely new level.

With so many witnesses to Lazarus' death and burial, and the verifiable evidence of his resurrection readily available to anyone visiting Bethany, many came to believe in Jesus as a result of this miracle. But that caused consternation in Jerusalem, and led to the authorities renewing and intensifying their resolve that Jesus should be put to death.

With this in view, the chief priests gave orders that if anyone knew where Jesus was, they should inform the authorities so that they might arrest Him. This put me in immediate danger. Under the new order, simply being with Jesus would be enough to indict me on a charge of obstructing justice, withholding information vital to an investigation, or aiding and abetting a known criminal.

I had become a follower of Jesus in the hope that this would be to my advantage, but it was now abundantly clear that I needed to reconsider what was in my best interests. For some time, I had felt a growing suspicion that I might be more at home in the company of Jesus' enemies than I was in the circle of His friends. The waste of the perfume at Bethany turned that thought into a settled conviction. It was time to move on.

5

Decision

Over the next four days, I thought carefully about my position. People who are successful in finance focus not on what is, but on what soon will be. I had developed that art, and, in my best judgment, what would soon be was that Jesus was going down. I wanted to make sure that I would not go down with Him.

It was not an easy calculation. What happened to Lazarus led to a new surge of enthusiasm for Jesus. This was clear for all to see when, a couple of days later, people lined the Mount of Olives, cheering and waving palm branches as they hailed Jesus as the Son of David.

But people are fickle, and I knew better than to project the future based on passing enthusiasm. Power does not lie with the people, but with those who control the levers of government.

I remember thinking, while I walked with the others behind Jesus on that donkey, that this outpouring of adulation, added as it was to the surge of enthusiasm that had followed the raising of Lazarus, would inevitably strengthen the resolve of the authorities to do away with Jesus.

Every movement has its moment and, to my mind, Jesus had missed His best opportunity. If He had embraced the crowd when they wanted to proclaim Him as king, He would have had a solid base on which to build. And if He had then added the crowds drawn by the resurrection of Lazarus, He might have reached a tipping point in which He could overwhelm the Jewish authorities, take His seat in the temple, and proclaim Himself to be God. But that opportunity had been squandered, and, despite the cheers of the crowds, Jesus was now in a vulnerable position.

I decided that the time was right for me to make my move. Having given three years of my life to what I now saw as a failed enterprise, I was determined to get some return from the investment I had made. By being in the inner circle, I had access to what the priests wanted and desperately needed—intel about the movements of Jesus. Information is power, and I figured that what I had was worth a great deal.

Slipping away from the other disciples, I made my way to the palace of the High Priest. When I knocked, a servant, whose name I later found out was Malchus, came to the door. I told him that I had information that would be highly prized by his master, that it concerned Jesus, and that I was ready to make a deal.

Malchus told me that I had come at a good time since the chief priests, the elders, and the Pharisees were all present in the house. He told me to wait in the hall and said that he would relay my message.

I waited anxiously, knowing that what I was about to do was laden with risk. I had no intention of revealing my identity until I had a firm deal in place that included immunity from prosecution, but, despite the risk of what I was about to do, I knew that the alternative would expose me to greater peril. To remain as a disciple of Jesus when all my instincts told me that He was going down would, I thought, have been the greatest folly.

After a few minutes, a large group of priests, dressed in their full regalia, marched down the hall, ushered me into a small room, and closed the door. They were wise enough not to ask my name and came straight to the point of our mutual interest.

'Now, what is this information about Jesus that you think would be of interest to us?'

I decided to answer their question with one of my own.

'What will you give me if I deliver Him over to you?'

They looked at each other with surprise and with obvious interest.

Ignoring my question about the money, they focused on clarifying the offer I had just made. One of them repeated my words slowly so that each of them seemed to hang in the air: 'You... can... deliver... Him... to us?' 'Yes,' I said.

'How will you do that?'

'I will need a full cohort of soldiers, and they will need to be armed,' I said. 'I will lead you to where He will be, and I can identify Him for you so you will be sure there is no mistake.'

It was clear to me that their interest was engaged.

'We can't arrest Him when He is surrounded by a crowd,' one of them said.

'Which is almost always,' said another.

'And we can't arrest Him during the feast,' said a third. 'If we did, there would be uproar among the people.'

'There are still two days before the feast,' I said, 'and you can trust me to find a time and a place where you can arrest Him without having any trouble from the people. I know who He is and where He goes.'

I could see that they were sold on my proposal, and knew it was time to close the deal.

'So, how much will you give me?' I asked, again.

I reckoned it was to my advantage to invite an offer from them rather than propose a price myself, and knowing the value of what I had laid before them, I hoped that they would offer a sizeable sum that would keep me in style for the rest of my life. But in this I was greatly mistaken.

'We will give you thirty pieces of silver.'

My face drained and my blood ran cold. Thirty pieces of silver was the kind of money you paid for a common slave! I was stunned by this lowball offer.

I considered demanding a higher price. Then it hit me: I was trapped. By going to the priests, I had exposed myself as one of Jesus' circle. If I had walked away, I would have been a marked man, and, at some point, when they finally caught up with Jesus, they would have it in for me.

Besides, it was not at all obvious that I had the option of walking away. I was alone in the house of the High Priest, and no one knew where I was. They had the power to arrest me, and if that had been their choice, I would have disappeared without trace.

I had arrived confident that the initiative was in my hands. I left knowing that the power was in theirs. Having begun with thoughts of making my fortune, I quickly realized that my priority was simply to survive. So, without commenting on their insulting offer, I simply said: 'Fine. But whatever happens, I want your word that I will have complete immunity from any charges in any of the courts that you oversee.'

To this they agreed.

Without further words, I left the palace, and, once in the street, breathed a huge sigh of relief.

After making the deal, the last thing I wanted was to rejoin Jesus and the disciples. The more you enter into sympathy with the enemies of Jesus, the less you have in common with His friends. But, to fulfill the promise I had made to the priests, I needed to know Jesus' movements, and, for that reason, I went back to join Him for what proved to be His Last Supper.

I also knew that if I had been missing on such an occasion, I would have drawn attention to myself. The others would have known that something was wrong, and, if that happened, the opportunity to keep my side of the bargain with the priests would be gone.

Two days had passed since I had made the deal, and I was pressed to find a time and place where Jesus would be away from the crowds. Night would be ideal, and, with families all over the city at home for the Passover feast, I figured that this night might be my opportunity.

There was tension in the air when we gathered in an upper room to celebrate the Passover with Jesus. To understand what happened, you have to picture how we sat when gathered around the table.

Forget chairs. We didn't have those. The table was low, just a forearm's height from the floor. We reclined in a circle around it, each of us leaning on his left arm and eating from the table with his right hand.

The host sat at the head of the table, and the most honored guests would sit at his right and his left, with the rest taking their places down the sides of the table. Jesus spoke about this on one occasion, telling us not to choose a place of honor for ourselves, lest the host should ask us to move further down the table. Instead, Jesus said, we should choose the lowest place. The host, He said, may then call you to move up higher.

The disciples must not have recalled this, because when we gathered, an argument blew up over which of them was the greatest and who should sit closest to Jesus. Where people sat when they gathered for an occasion like the Passover was a big deal, and this really got them going.

When the time came for us to take our places at the table, Jesus motioned to John to sit on His right and then, to my great surprise, He invited me to sit on His left. 'Let the greatest among you become as the youngest, and the leader as one who serves,' He said. Then, as we took our places reclining at the table, He got up, tied a towel around His waist and, pouring water into a basin, knelt down and began to wash our feet.

Washing feet was the kind of thing that only the lowest servant would do. When Jesus became the servant, our argument was ended and our pride was humbled. There was nothing more to debate.

First, Jesus washed the feet of John, then Thomas, and Andrew, and Matthew. The room was silent as Jesus made His way around the circle. But when He came to Peter, the tension of that silence was broken.

'You shall never wash my feet,' Peter said.

'If I do not wash you, you have no share with me,' Jesus replied.

Peter, who so often swung from one extreme to another, said, 'Lord, not only my feet but also my hands and my head!'

That led Jesus to say something that made me really anxious. Looking beyond Peter to the whole group, He said: 'You are clean, but not every one of you.'

Not all of you are clean. What did He mean?

After washing the feet of Peter, Jesus continued around the table until, having begun with John on His right, He ended with me on His left. Taking my feet in His hands, He looked up into my eyes. I wanted to look away but knew that if I did, I would betray myself. No words were spoken, but there was love for me in the eyes of Jesus—genuine love that I could neither doubt nor avoid.

Taking His place at the head of the table between John and myself, Jesus became visibly troubled. 'Truly, truly, I say to you, one of you will betray me,' He said.

A sense of shock descended on the whole group, and, realizing the danger of the moment, I did my best not to react except to share the sense of astonishment that had come across the room. Thankfully, reclining immediately next to Jesus, I was hidden from His line of sight as He looked down the table.

Gathering my thoughts, I assured myself that there was no way Jesus or any of the others could know about the deal I had made with the priests. And even if Jesus had perceived that one of us would betray Him, there were others in the group to whom the finger of suspicion would point before it got to me.

Jesus had spoken before about how one of the inner circle was a devil, and I had reason to believe He was talking about Peter. All of us were present on that unforgettable occasion when Jesus had spoken about how He would suffer and die. Peter rejected what He was saying completely, but Jesus turned on him and looking directly at Peter, He said: 'Get behind me, Satan.'

These shocking words could hardly have been clearer. Peter had become the agent of Satan, and so it was no surprise to me when, some time later, Jesus had said: 'One of you is a devil.' Knowing Peter's temperament, I could easily imagine him being the betrayer, and since that possibility was clear to me, it would be clear to the others and also, I assumed, to Jesus. So, even when He announced that one of us would betray Him, I still felt confident that my secret was intact.

Sorrow spread around the circle as we all tried to take in the weight of what Jesus had just said: 'One of you will betray me.'

As usual, Peter was the first to break the silence. 'Lord, is it I?' he asked.

Jesus made no answer.

Then John asked the same question: 'Lord, is it I?'

The question seemed to move around the circle: James, Thomas, Andrew, and Matthew, each of them wanting to know if he was the one. But Jesus made no answer.

Two things struck me: First, no one asked, 'Is it Judas?' That reassured me. Second, they all seemed to feel that they had it in them to let their Lord down. Knowing the corruption of their own hearts, none of them felt that treachery was beyond them.

Then Jesus said some words that have stayed with me ever since: 'Woe to that man by whom the Son of Man is betrayed! It would have been better for that man if he had not been born.'

Distracted by this thought for a moment, I snapped back into reality and realized that I would draw attention to myself if I did not join the others in asking, 'Lord, is it I?' So, wanting to make sure that I was not the last to ask, I touched Jesus on His left shoulder, and whispered in His ear, 'Is it I, Rabbi?'

With Jesus making no response to any of the others, no one was paying attention when I asked my question, and the answer Jesus gave to me was spoken so softly that only I could have heard it. Turning toward me, and speaking just a few inches from my ear, Jesus replied: 'You have said so.'

A few moments later, Bartholomew raised his voice from the far end of the table, and asked 'Lord, is it I?' This was the eighth time that the same question had been asked, and as far as the other disciples were aware, Jesus had made no response. The thought of the other four all asking the same question was too much for Peter, so he cut to the chase, and motioned to John, who was sitting to the right of Jesus: 'Ask Him who it is!'

Fear gripped me.

I knew why Peter was asking. Jesus had said that someone in the room was about to betray Him and Peter wanted to know who it was so that he could deal with the problem by eliminating that person.

When I arrived at the supper, I had noticed two swords, one of them Peter's, ominously placed in the corner of the room. I knew that if, at that moment, Jesus had said to John, 'Tell Peter it is Judas,' Peter would have drawn his sword and run me through right then and there.

I held my breath as John leaned back against Jesus, and asked, 'Who is it, Lord?'

Jesus answered so softly that no one other than John to His right and I to His left could hear the answer. 'It is he to whom I will give this morsel of bread when I have dipped it.' Then, Jesus dipped the bread and, turning around, offered it to me.

When a host offered bread, it was a sign of friendship, and, as Jesus extended His hand, I felt His love reaching out to me again. For a fleeting moment, the thought occurred to me that I could say to Him: 'Jesus, I have something to confess: I have felt the pull of evil; I have been stealing money from the bag. I have made a deal with the priests and taken money to betray you. Please have mercy on me.' But I steeled myself against this thought and, remaining silent, I took the bread that He had offered.

As I ate the bread, I knew that I had crossed another line, but I was strengthened by a determined resolve that seemed to come on me at critical moments in my journey. I had felt it first when I had gone to the priests, and I felt it again as I took the morsel of bread from Jesus.

Looking back, I now see that Satan launched a relentless assault on my soul. If that makes you feel sorry for me, please spare me your pity. Satan seeks the destruction of every follower of Jesus, and his assaults on me were no different from what he attempts with any other disciple.

Satan can only enter a person's life when that person opens the door. I had opened my life to the enemy through my persistent refusal to repent, and Satan entered through the door I had opened. Every time I sinned, and refused to confess, my sin acquired greater power over my soul until, in the end, I lost all trace of the desire I once had known to follow after Jesus.

'What you are going to do, do quickly,' Jesus said to me. There was no doubt about His meaning. I had made my decision, and Jesus was dismissing me from the room. I got up and left, without looking back.

What the others made of this, I never knew. Since I had the money, they might easily have assumed that Jesus had sent me out to buy something for the feast. John was the only one who knew why I was leaving. He alone had heard what Jesus had said about the morsel of bread.

So now I was outside the circle, excluded and no longer welcome.

'To hell with it,' I thought. 'They don't want me and I don't want them.' I walked out into the night knowing that I was finally done with Jesus.

6

Defection

My time in the upper room was well spent, because now I had all the information I needed to fulfill my promise to the priests. I had learned that, after the supper, Jesus would go to a garden outside the city. I knew the place well because Jesus had often met with us there. It was a quiet place at any time of day, but at night it would be completely deserted.

Armed with the knowledge of where Jesus would soon be, I made my way across the city to the High Priest's palace. Again, it was Malchus who opened the door.

'Round up the men,' I said.

Without asking for any further information, he was gone, leaving me alone in the hall where I had been when I first came to make the deal.

Rounding up the temple guard was easy. The High Priest had a clear and effective chain of command, and it was not long before these officers arrived in the hall.

But the arrest of Jesus was only the first step in a plan that the priests had thought through carefully. They were seeking the death penalty, which only the Romans had the power to invoke, and so it was important for the priests that the arrest should be made in cooperation and collaboration with the forces of Rome that were based at the Antonia fortress, close to the High Priest's palace.

Word was sent, and in less than an hour, the entire force had been assembled. The front line, behind Malchus and myself, was made up of the temple officers who served the High Priest. Some of them arrived with swords and clubs. Others carried torches and lanterns. Behind them was the cohort of Roman soldiers I had asked for. A full cohort would have been six hundred men, and, although I did not count them, I could see that the force they had sent was more than sufficient for any scenario.

'Are you sure that such a large force is really necessary?' Malchus asked me.

'Malchus, I have seen Him slip away from large crowds when people have tried to seize Him before. We don't want to take any chances.'

My plan was meticulous. I had thought of everything. If the disciples resisted Jesus' arrest, we were armed with swords and clubs. If Jesus chose to hide in the garden, we had torches and lanterns and would search until we found Him. Our force was overwhelming in numbers and strength and, without the presence of the crowd to protect Him, I was certain that our mission would end in success.

When everyone was gathered, Malchus called the group to order. He reminded them of the importance of our mission and then invited me to give instructions.

'We are heading to the Garden of Gethsemane,' I said. 'Jesus will be there with His eleven disciples. Apart from them, the place should be deserted.'

Then I told them about the sign. One of the priests' biggest concerns was that, in the darkness, one of the disciples might step forward, identifying himself as Jesus, and that we would arrest the wrong man, allowing Jesus to slip away into the night. The priests needed me not only to take them to the right place, but also to make sure that they arrested the right man.

I knew that if I relied on pointing to Jesus in the darkness, there would be room for confusion, especially if the disciples started running in different directions. So I settled on a sign that could not be mistaken. 'When we arrive in the garden, I will identify Him with a kiss,' I said. A nod and grunt of approval went around the group. 'When I kiss Him,' I continued, 'you must arrest Him immediately. No delays. And when you seize Him, make sure that you hold Him securely. Whatever you do, don't underestimate Him. I have seen Him still a storm and even raise the dead'

Some of the Roman soldiers at the back seemed to find this amusing. Here we were, a great crowd, fully armed, setting out on a mission to arrest one man who had the support of no more than eleven friends. The size of the force and the intensity of my instructions seemed ludicrous to the professionals, who must have wondered why we were mounting what looked like a major operation to accomplish something so apparently simple. But then, they didn't know Jesus.

With our preparations complete, we set out—Jew and Gentile united together—the power of religion and the power of the state moving as one with the objective of arresting and binding Jesus.

It was an overwhelming force, and I was leading them. Me! Judas Iscariot! The one who was always named last among the disciples! Now I was at the front, striding out with a vast armed force behind me, all of them following my lead. My moment had finally come.

When we arrived at Gethsemane, I could see the disciples scattered across the garden. It looked to me as if they had been sleeping, and were still in the process of getting to their feet.

What took me by surprise was that Jesus came striding toward us. I had thought that I would have to seek Him out, but instead He stepped forward resolutely from the trees as if to confront us.

'Whom do you seek?' He demanded. His question was addressed to Malchus. This was not what I had expected. I had told the priests that I would go up to Jesus and kiss Him, but Jesus had seized the initiative, and now I was unsure of how to proceed.

Malchus responded to the question: 'Whom do we seek? Jesus of Nazareth,' he said.

What happened next was quite extraordinary and wholly unexpected. Jesus said: 'I am he.'

As He said this, we were overwhelmed by a blinding flash of light. It was so intense that our entire army—the priests, Pharisees, elders, and Roman soldiers, along with Malchus and myself—collapsed on the ground as if we had all been struck by a bolt of lightning.

I felt rather foolish lying there in the dust and, looking up, could see the surprise of the disciples. It must have been quite a sight: hundreds of armed men, with swords, clubs, lanterns and torches, all falling backward and landing on top of each other on the ground!

Who would have thought that a small group of twelve men would still be standing when a force of hundreds who had come to arrest one of them was lying on their backs in the dust? It was all rather embarrassing.

This was the kind of unexpected complication I had been afraid of. I had heard about something like it before, when Peter, James, and John had gone up a mountain with Jesus. The best they could do to describe what happened was to tell us that a powerful light radiated from Jesus. 'His face shone like the sun, and His clothes became white as light,' they said. I feared that something similar might be happening again.

After a few moments, I got up and brushed the dust from my clothing. Behind me, the temple guards picked up their torches, lanterns, swords, and clubs and behind them, the Roman cohort slowly got to their feet. None of them were laughing now.

When we were all back on our feet, Jesus repeated His question: 'Whom do you seek?'

Somewhat shaken, Malchus replied as he had before, 'Jesus of Nazareth,' he said.

'I told you that I am He,' Jesus answered, 'so, if you seek me, let these men go.'

I was struck by the fact that even in this moment of extreme danger, Jesus' first concern was for the good of His friends. The priests had been concerned that one of the disciples might give himself up in order to protect Jesus, but Jesus gave Himself up in order to protect them.

So far, nothing had gone according to plan. It had all seemed so simple: I would arrive with an overwhelming force, and identify Jesus with a kiss. The armed guards would then make the arrest, supported by the Roman cohort. Game over.

The reality was quite different. Jesus had seized the initiative and identified Himself. Through some outburst of power that I did not understand, we had all been knocked over, and, as soon as we had recovered, Jesus identified Himself for a second time.

The plan that called for me to identify Jesus with a kiss now seemed completely unnecessary.

But, in the absence of another plan, I went ahead anyway.

'Greetings, Rabbi,' I said, as I moved toward Him. But before I could reach Him, He responded with a question that still haunts me.

'Judas, would you betray the Son of Man with a kiss?'

Even in the garden, as I was about to betray Him, Jesus was reaching out to me in love. It was as if He were saying, 'Do you really want to do this, Judas? I have already identified myself to these men. I am giving myself into their hands. Nothing will be gained by your act of treachery. Judas, don't set yourself against me! Leave these men! Come under my protection! Step over the line right now and take your stand again with me, and with my disciples.'

I hesitated for a moment, but I had passed the point of no return. Ignoring His last plea, I took that final step forward, and kissed Him.

There is an old psalm that I learned as a boy. It describes a scene where rulers rage against God and against His anointed Messiah. They plot and plan because they want to get rid of Him. The psalm says that God laughs at these machinations, and somehow I think He was laughing when our entire army fell to the ground. The old psalm, calling us to make peace with God, then says: 'Kiss the Son, lest

He be angry.' Well, I kissed Him all right, but this was not the kiss of affection. It was the kiss of betrayal.

As I kissed Jesus, I heard the sound of sharpened metal as the armed guards behind me drew their swords, ready to make the arrest. I then felt a movement in the air, and realized that Peter had drawn his sword, too, raising it high above his head and bringing it down with a crushing blow on Malchus, who was standing just behind me.

There is no doubt in my mind that Peter intended to split the head of Malchus in two, but he missed by a few inches, and ended up taking off his ear. What possessed him to do this, I have no idea. His sword was no match for the armed force of hundreds that I was leading, and striking a blow against Malchus risked igniting a conflict that could only have ended in the slaughter of all the disciples.

Besides this, whatever had happened with that blazing light that caused all of us to fall over proved beyond question that, if He chose to, Jesus was well able to defend Himself against an army of any size.

I was relieved when Jesus intervened. 'No more of this!' He insisted, as He stepped between Malchus and Peter. Turning to Peter, He said:

'Put your sword back into its place. For all who take the sword will perish by the sword!'

We all drew breath, wondering what would happen next. 'Do you think that I cannot appeal to my Father, and He will at once send me more than twelve legions of angels?' Jesus asked. Then He added: 'Shall I not drink the cup that the Father has given me?'

It was clear to me that Jesus had already decided to hand Himself over to the authorities and that the act, for which I would always be remembered, would turn out to be one of supreme irrelevance.

I recalled how Jesus had said: 'No one takes my life from me, but I lay it down of my own accord. I have authority to lay it down and I have authority to take it up again.' Jesus was not arrested as a helpless victim. Having demonstrated the supreme power by which He controlled all that happened, He gave Himself willingly into the hands of His enemies.

That kiss was the most futile thing I ever did. I had thought of it as the centerpiece of my elaborate plan, but it accomplished nothing except to confirm my defection from being a follower of Jesus. The armed force was equally futile. I had brought an army of several hundred men, but in truth, a single arresting officer would have been enough.

Before giving Himself up, Jesus stooped down to the ground and picked up the ear that had been severed from Malchus' head. He placed it over the bleeding wound, holding it in the place from which it had been struck, and then, slowly, He removed His hand. To the astonishment of everyone nearby, the wound was completely healed.

Turning to the priests, elders, and Pharisees, Jesus said: 'Have you come out as against a robber, with swords and clubs to capture me? Day after day I was with you in the temple teaching, and you did not seize me. But let the Scriptures be fulfilled.' With this, Jesus stepped forward, presenting His wrists so that they could bind Him. As He did, the disciples ran off into the night.

The arrest was made jointly by the Roman cohort and by the officers of the temple. Watching them bind Him, I remembered the man possessed by evil spirits who had been bound in chains because he was a threat to the community. The power that possessed him was so great that he had been able to break the chains, and no one was able to bind him anymore. Jesus had delivered that man, demonstrating beyond any doubt that His power was stronger than the chains. Now, the priests were binding Jesus, and Jesus was allowing them to do it.

The group I had been leading took Jesus to the High Priest's palace, but once they had their man, they had no further use for me. And since the disciples had already fled, I was left alone in the garden to reflect on all that had transpired.

Despite repeated appeals from Jesus, I had embraced rebellion, and chosen to defy Him. Yet my treachery did nothing to deter Him. Giving Himself into the hands of His enemies was exactly what He had intended.

7

Contrition

I had been picturing a scene of celebration in which, with Jesus under arrest, I would receive a hero's welcome in the palace of the High Priest. The long hall where I had waited would be lined with the elders, the chief priests, and the Pharisees, cheering and chanting my name. I imagined myself being ushered into the presence of the High Priest who, rising from his chair would say, 'Well done! You have been a good servant, and we will put you in charge of many things.'

The reality was very different. Left alone in the garden, I settled down under some trees in the vain hope of getting some sleep. Over and over, the events that had just transpired played out in my mind.

When I closed my eyes, the blinding light that had knocked us to the ground flashed across my mind. I remembered that Jesus had warned us: 'Whoever is ashamed of me and of my words... of him will the Son of Man be ashamed when he comes in the glory of his Father with the holy angels.' Could that bolt of lightning have been the glory of the Father breaking out from Jesus?

Closing my eyes again, I saw the hand of Jesus holding that severed ear to the head of Malchus, and heard Him saying: 'Love your enemies, and pray for those who persecute you.' Then came the memories of others who had been healed in these early days when I had first followed Jesus: Peter's mother-in law, the crowds of people with all kinds of illness at Capernaum, and that man, lowered from the roof by his friends, to whom Jesus had said: 'Pick up your bed, and go home!'

There was an authority in the voice of Jesus. I heard it again in the garden when He commanded Peter to put away his sword, preventing the slaughter of His disciples. How strange, I thought, that He should say this to the disciple who sought to defend Him and not to the enemies who sought to arrest Him.

As these thoughts of Jesus' authority, His power, and what I now believed was an unveiling of His glory ran through my mind, I was gripped with a growing sense of fear and foreboding. *What have I done?*

To my great surprise, these thoughts also gave me a lifeline of hope. *Jesus had said to Peter in the garden that He could appeal to His Father who would send, at once, more than twelve legions of angels. If that was true why, after knocking our entire army to the ground, had Jesus given Himself up so willingly? If He could call on twelve thousand angels, why did He not do so? It made no sense. Unless...*

A new thought began to form in my mind. *Perhaps the blinding flash of light in the garden was a foretaste of what was to come? Could it be that Jesus was planning the greatest display of His glory? Could it be that He would call in the angels when He was brought to trial and that they would vindicate Him as the Son of God, bringing both His enemies and His friends to confess Him as their Messiah? If that was His plan, it would be a masterstroke, and it would be an event not to be missed.*

There were still some hours to go before sunrise, but I knew that the priests would want to move quickly. I also knew that whatever judicial process the priests may have followed they would, in the end, have to hand Jesus over to the Romans, since they alone had the authority to impose the death penalty.

Since executions typically happened early in the morning, I figured that they would bring Jesus to the governor before sunrise. With these thoughts in my mind, I left the garden, made my way into the city, and headed for the home of Pontius Pilate.

When I arrived, I saw the same priests, elders, and Pharisees I had led a few hours before. They were gathered outside Pilate's residence, and Pilate himself was standing at the gate with them. Though I stayed hidden behind the delegation, I managed to get close enough to hear what was being said.

'What accusation do you bring against this man?' Pilate asked. I could tell that he was irritated, which was not surprising given that he had clearly been awakened in the night.

'If this man were not doing evil, we would not have delivered him over to you,' said one of the priests.

Pilate was a shrewd man, and he quickly realized that the priests' dispute with Jesus was most likely a religious one, belonging to their jurisdiction rather than his. 'Take him yourselves and judge him by your own law,' Pilate said.

That forced the priests to get to the point: 'It is not lawful for us to put anyone to death,' they said.

Realizing that they needed to bring a charge that would engage Pilate's interest, the priests advanced a new accusation. 'We found this man misleading our nation and forbidding us to give tribute to Caesar, and saying that he himself is Christ, a king,' they said.

Pilate looked skeptical. My guess was that he saw this as a local matter, and he wasn't at all convinced that he should have been bothered in the night.

After questioning Jesus in the presence of the priests, Pilate announced that he found no charge to bring against Him. But the priests pressed their case more urgently. 'He stirs up the people, teaching throughout all Judea, from Galilee even to this place,' they said.

The reference to Galilee opened up a way for Pilate to settle the unwelcome issue that had been brought before him. Galilee was in the jurisdiction of Herod the Tetrarch, who was staying at his residence in Jerusalem, which was not more than a few minutes' walk from where we were standing. So, Pilate sent Jesus over to Herod.

The priests had no choice but to follow Pilate's direction, so they went, with Jesus still bound, as He had been in the garden. But the speed with which they all returned told me both that little of significance had happened in the time with Herod, and that the priests, having complied with Pilate's direction, were eager to return and press their case further with the Governor.

But Pilate was in no mood for being pushed around. Convening the chief priests together, he reviewed what had happened. 'You brought me this man as one who was misleading the people,' he said. 'And after examining him before you, I did not find this man guilty of any of your charges against him.' He then pointed out that Herod was clearly of the same opinion, since he had sent Jesus back. The case was clear: 'Nothing deserving death has been done by him,' he said.

Then, Pilate came up with a proposal that he thought would finally settle the issue. It had become a tradition that during the Passover, Pilate would release a prisoner, chosen by popular demand. Since the choice was in the hands of the people, he brought out Barabbas, a prisoner whose violence was so notorious that nobody in their right mind would want him back on their streets. In a stroke of genius, he asked the crowd to choose between Barabbas and Jesus.

I thought for a moment that Jesus would go free. Surely, no one would request the release of Barabbas. But the chief priests and the elders moved quickly through the crowd, persuading the people to ask for Barabbas and call for the crucifixion of Jesus.

By the time the Governor repeated his question, the crowd was calling for Barabbas. Clearly taken by surprise, Pilate asked: 'Then what shall I do with Jesus who is called Christ?' At this the whole crowd shouted as one: 'Let him be crucified!'

Pilate pressed the crowd: 'Why, what evil has he done?' But this seemed to incite the crowd even more, and I could see that the Governor had the makings of a riot on his hands.

He brought out a bowl of water and rather pretentiously washed his hands as an indication that he was having nothing further to do with the case. 'I am innocent of this man's blood,' he said.

Pilate was ready to move on. But as a shrewd politician, he knew that merely absolving himself of responsibility would do nothing to appease the crowd. He also knew that that the best resolution to this dispute would be one that had something in it for all sides. So, having pronounced Jesus innocent of any offence that would warrant death, he offered something to placate the anger of the priests: He would have Jesus flogged and then would release Him.

I chose not to watch the flogging, but waited near the Governor's residence to see what would happen when it was done. Eventually, Pilate appeared. 'I am bringing him out to you,' he said, 'that you may know that I find no guilt in him.'

I froze with shock as Jesus was dragged out by two soldiers and paraded in front of the people. His face was so bloodied and bruised that He was barely recognizable. A mock crown, made with branches from a thorn bush, twisted together, had been pressed onto His head, and a faded purple robe had been draped over His body, lampooning the claim that He was a king.

'Behold the man!' Pilate said, with a dramatic sweep of his hand.

Do it now! I said to myself. *This is the moment! Call in the legion of angels! Heal your own wounds as you healed the ear of Malchus! Throw Pilate and this entire crowd to the ground by unveiling your glory as you did in the garden!* But none of that happened.

It seemed clear to me that, having already been pushed beyond what he thought was right in having Jesus flogged, Pilate would allow himself to be pushed no further, and was determined to release Jesus. But the crowd had become even stronger in its resolve. Someone stepped forward and shouted: 'If you release this man, you are not Caesar's friend.' The crowd roared in approval, and called again for Jesus to be crucified.

Pilate was getting nowhere. When he pursued justice and pronounced Jesus innocent, the priests brought new and different charges. When he reassigned the case to Herod, Jesus was quickly sent back. When he appealed to the goodwill of the people, they chose to release a murderer, and when he sought compromise by having Jesus flogged, the crowd still called for Him to be crucified. With all other options exhausted, it was clear to me that Pilate faced a choice between appeasing the crowd and risking a full-scale riot. I waited to see his next move.

Walking to the Stone Pavement, a small platform in front of the Governor's residence that was used for legal declarations, Pilate sat down and pronounced the judgment that for the last few hours he had been trying to avoid: 'Jesus of Nazareth is sentenced to death by crucifixion.'

When I saw that Jesus had been condemned, I knew that my last hope of being released from the effects of what I had done was gone. As I listened to Pilate's repeated assertion that Jesus had done nothing wrong, I wondered what had made me think I was right to betray Him. To my surprise, no offence came to mind. I had betrayed Him because His agenda did not align with mine.

I realized that I had played a part in that most heinous of crimes: shedding innocent blood.

A wave of contrition overwhelmed me. I was seized with regret, and I knew what I had to do. *I must confess. I must take ownership for the wrong I have done. I must tell the priests that Pilate was right. Jesus has done nothing wrong, and I have been involved in a great miscarriage of justice.*

What I had done could not be undone. My sin was irreversible and restitution was impossible. But I had to disassociate myself from what I had done. So, as Jesus was led out of the city to the hill where the Romans executed their victims, I made my way back to the house of the High Priest. As I walked, I felt the weight of the thirty pieces of silver in my tunic. The money felt filthy to me, and I was desperate to get rid of it.

By the time I arrived at the house of the High Priest, it was about the third hour after sunrise. By that time, Jesus would have arrived at the place of execution, and they would be nailing Him to the cross. I tried to put that out of my mind and focus on the matter at hand: I had to find a priest. I needed to confess. I longed for absolution.

When Malchus opened the door, he seemed surprised to see me. 'Malchus,' I said, 'I have committed a great evil. Let me speak to the priests.' I hoped that, having been miraculously healed by Jesus, Malchus would have sympathy with my change of heart. I was not disappointed.

He told me that some of the priests were on duty at the temple. 'The others,' he said, 'went to the Governor's residence, and since they have not returned, I assume they have gone to witness the crucifixion.'

Malchus said that he would come to the temple with me, and so, together, we made the short journey through the narrow streets. When we arrived in the courtyard, Malchus told me to wait at the door while he went in to gather as many of the chief priests and elders as he could find.

I waited outside the temple, and, eventually, a small group of elders and priests came to the door. They seemed surprised to see me and did not invite me in.

'I have sinned,' I said, 'by betraying innocent blood.'

Before I could continue my confession, one of the elders cut me off. 'What is that to us?' he said.

I was about to point out that they were priests, that I was carrying an unbearable burden of guilt, and that hearing confession was part of their work, but I could see that as far as they were concerned, our conversation was over.

I was on my own. And then it dawned on me: *these priests have nothing to offer that will help me deal with my sins. They have blood on their own hands as well!*

I no longer wanted them or their money. Taking the bag from my tunic, I threw the silver I had been paid into the temple. As the open bag landed, the coins scattered on the stone floor and, without any further word, I turned my back on them and walked away in disgust.

Words that Jesus had spoken pounded through my mind as I made my way out of the city: 'Woe to that man by whom the Son of Man is betrayed. It would have been better for that man if he had not been born.' I was that man. I wished I had never been born.

The Messiah, I had always believed, would be the light and hope of our people. But I had put out that light, and now I was without hope. Having conspired with others in a crime for which restitution could not be made, I now carried a burden of guilt that no priest and no prayers could relieve.

I remembered how Jesus had said to that paralyzed man lowered through the roof: 'Your sins are forgiven.' At the time, I thought the miracle of his getting up to walk was the greater gift, but as I made my way from the temple, I would have given anything to hear the voice of Jesus say: 'Your sins are forgiven.' But He was gone, and that now seemed impossible to me.

With the weight of my own folly pressing down on me, I made my way to a piece of property I had bought some time before with money taken from the common purse entrusted to me by Jesus and the disciples. It was a small field on a high ridge, bordered by a cliff that dropped down to an open expanse below, and at the edge of the cliff there was a tree.

Having fixed a rope to a branch of that tree, I looked up at the sun, and realized from its position that it must have been about midday. Then, to my complete astonishment, everything was plunged into darkness. I had never seen anything like this before, and, feeling certain that this must be the judgment of God, I jumped from the ledge on which I was standing.

The last thing I remember was the sound of the branch to which I had tied the rope breaking. I fell into the darkness, and I feel that I have been falling ever since.

8

Reflection

When I died, I left my body behind in the field. I am a spirit now, a spirit shivering in the darkness.

I often wish that I could sleep. Unconsciousness would be a welcome relief from this miserable existence, but sleep never comes. I am fully conscious, and I am always awake. My mind never stops. Round and round I go, pondering my past life, loathing my present misery, and knowing that none of this will ever end.

I now understand what Jesus was referring to when He spoke about gnashing of teeth. My

experience down here is one of perpetual dis-
content, in which I find that I am always angry
and never at peace, always frustrated and never
satisfied.

The only time there is laughter here is when we
mock the new arrivals. The greater they were in
the world, the more they suffer our scorn. When
those who were once rich and famous show up,
we say, 'Now you are just like the rest of us. All
of your power and all of your money are gone,
and you have become weak, just like us!'

The great irony of my existence here is that,
though I cannot be happy in hell, I could not be
happy in heaven either. Heaven is a holy place, and
all of the people there are holy. Jesus is the center
of their life and their joy. Why those who find no
joy in Him on earth would imagine that He would
be a joy to them in heaven is quite beyond me.

What I became on earth is what I am now,
and though I live with unending regret over my
sins against God, I have no desire to be recon-
ciled to Him. I see now why hell is forever.
After all the time that has passed since I came
here, I remain as I was when I arrived: resolute
in my resistance to God, despite knowing that
this continuing battle leads only to my ever-
increasing loss.

It may surprise you to know that I am more
profoundly aware of Jesus down here than I ever

was during the years that I followed Him on earth. I abandoned my faith because I wanted to be free from the demands of following Jesus, but now I find that the knowledge of His reign and His rule is unavoidable. I took my life because I wanted to escape from what I had done, but now I feel the weight of it more than ever.

So, why did I miss out on heaven? You need to know first, that it was not because I took my own life. This, of course, added both to my sins and to my misery. Taking my life was, like betraying Jesus, an irreversible sin. It was, and always is, the ultimate act of defiance against the God who gives life. It is also an ultimate act of folly. I took my life because I wanted to end my misery and escape the consequences of what I had done, but what I did only brought me into greater misery in this place where consequences cannot be escaped. Yet, sinful and foolish though it was, this sin against the sixth commandment was not, in itself, the reason I missed out on heaven.

You also need to know that the reason I missed out on heaven was not that I betrayed Jesus. Although that was a wicked and evil deed for which I am duly punished, I was not the only one to betray Him. The word 'betray' means to violate a trust that was given. Now, ask yourself honestly: Have you ever violated a trust that was given to you? Of course you have! We are all, in some way, traitors to the trust we have been given.

Then, you need to know that I did not miss out on heaven because I was somehow destined for hell from the beginning. When Jesus said: 'One of you is a devil,' He described what I became. I was not a devil when He chose me. Satan entered into me through a series of choices in which I opened a door to evil in my life.

To understand my story, you need to grasp that I was not a victim and I was not a pawn. I knew exactly what I was doing. I picked my side and I made my choice. Time after time, Jesus reached out to me, but I refused to listen. There is only one person to blame for my being in hell, and his name is Judas Iscariot.

So, why did I miss out on heaven, when for three years I followed and served Jesus? The answer is surprisingly simple: I gave up on Jesus.

As long as you are with Him, you have hope, but if you leave Him, you lose everything. Believe me. I know.

When I first met Jesus, I was drawn to Him. When I prayed, I was sincere. When I preached, I believed what I was saying. But, having started out as a disciple, I turned back and abandoned the faith I had once professed.

Giving up on Jesus was my downfall, but that choice was the outcome of other choices and patterns that shaped the person I became. Of these, there are three that are always on my mind.

First, looking back on my life as a disciple, I can see that it was all about myself. I followed Jesus because I thought that attaching myself to Him would give me a shot at making my mark in the world. Despite all I learned from Jesus, that never changed, and, in the end, I abandoned Jesus for the same reason I had joined Him: the love of self.

My relationship with Jesus was all about me. When He gave me what I wanted, I was with Him, but when following Him became hard and costly, I moved on.

Mixed motives of various sorts are woven together in all of our lives, but I was drawn to Jesus as a means to an end. Those who try to use Him to fulfill their own agenda always sell out on Him in the end.

Second, I opened up my life to Satan without realizing the destructive power he would wield over my soul. This began when I first stole money from the bag. I knew it was wrong, but I suppressed my conscience and carried on. As time passed, I found that I was able to hear the teaching of Jesus and even engage in ministry without feeling that I had any sins to confess or any need of His grace.

With this growing insensitivity to sin in my life, I became increasingly resistant to Jesus. When He spoke to me, I hardened my heart, and as I did, it was easier for me to shut out His voice until, in the end, I became completely unresponsive to His love.

Third, though I became contrite, I never pursued repentance. Yes, I went to the priests and made a full confession, telling them plainly that I had sinned. I was more sorry for betraying Jesus than I can ever put into words. But it was only the sorrow of regret.

Repentance is more than being sorry for what you have done. At its heart, it involves looking to Jesus and finding forgiveness in Him. Regret leads a person to look inward and despair. Repentance leads a person to look upward and find hope.

Attempting to use Jesus as a means to an end, opening my life up to the power of Satan, and indulging regret without pursuing repentance were all signs that I would not end up in heaven. But if you ask me to tell you in a single phrase why I am in hell, I say again, it was because I gave up on Jesus.

And here's why I say that: If, like the other disciples, I had remained a follower of Jesus, all of these other failings could have been forgiven. My selfish heart could have been changed. Satan's power in my life could have been broken, and, instead of remaining in the misery of regret, I could have found, in Jesus, the gift of repentance. But my choices led me in a different direction.

Looking back on my years as a follower of Jesus, I have arrived at this firm conclusion: if you get close to Him, one of two things will happen. Either you will become wholly His, or else you will slingshot away from Him, and end up farther from Him than you would have been if you had never known Him at all.

It is no longer a surprise to me that among those who hate Jesus the most are not a few who once professed to trust Him. Down here, I have seen some surprising cases of people who were raised in church but then, like me, abandoned the faith they once professed. Now they are locked into an unending antagonism toward God.

The claims of Jesus are so exclusive and His demands so pervasive that if you do not give yourself to Him completely, you will, in the end, give Him up altogether. There is no middle ground. Only those who have never known Jesus can remain indifferent to Him. Once you get close, the only alternatives are to fully love Him or to finally loathe Him.

Postscript

Q & A with author Colin S. Smith

Q1: Why did you write this book?
I wrote this book for people who are moving away from the faith they once professed.

Their number is growing fast. In 1990, about 8 per cent of Americans did not identify with any religion. By 2008, that number had doubled to 15 per cent and just four years later, it had risen to 20 per cent. Dubbed the 'nones', these people, when asked if they were Baptist, Catholic, Methodist, Presbyterian, Anglican, or Lutheran, or, more broadly, Christian, Muslim, or Hindu, answered 'None of the above.'

Behind this astonishing rise in people professing no religious affiliation is a growing trend of people who had at one time identified themselves as 'Christian' giving up on the faith they once professed in Jesus Christ.

But I have been moved to write by faces rather than numbers: the face of a young person brought up in a Christian home who now has little interest in the faith he once professed; the face of one who extended herself in Christian ministry but was disappointed and now is close to leaving the church; the face of one for whom life has brought pain and perplexity to the point where, having once given testimony to God's grace, he now wonders why he should believe in Christ at all.

I wrote this book to plead with you not to walk away from Jesus Christ.

Q2: If Judas is in hell, why would he be telling us the truth about Jesus?

My thinking about how Judas might tell his story has been guided by our Lord's story of the rich man and Lazarus (Luke 16:19-31).

The rich man had a clear memory of the events of his life, and so I have assumed that Judas could accurately recall what he saw, heard, and felt throughout his years as a follower of Jesus. Judas knew the truth even if, in the end, he did not believe or obey it.

I have also given weight to the request of the rich man that a message be sent to his brothers to warn them, lest they also come to the place of torment. This has led me to conclude that a person in hell might have some desire that others would be saved from the plight they experience.

Hell involves weeping and gnashing of teeth (Matt. 8:12), which indicates sorrow, regret, self-recrimination, and self-condemnation over decisions made and opportunities missed.

In the light of this, I think it is likely that Judas would have some wistfulness in recalling happier days of his life, along with the misery of reflecting on the path he ultimately chose.

Q3: Don't you think that Judas might be in heaven?

The thought behind this frequently asked question is that Judas may have repented at the last moment of his life and that, if he did, he would have been forgiven.

That he would have been forgiven is undoubtedly true. God's grace is sufficient to cover every sin, even the sin of betraying Christ. God offers this grace to every person, and Christ's forgiveness can be received at any time, even the last moment of a person's life.

This wonderful truth may allow some room for hope for those who grieve over loved ones who lived without evidence of either love or loyalty toward Jesus Christ. But in the case of Judas, the words of Jesus point in a different direction.

Jesus repeatedly distinguished been Judas and the other disciples. '*Did I not choose you, the twelve? And yet one of you is a devil,*' He said, and John explains that: '*He spoke of Judas, the son of Simon Iscariot, for he, one of the twelve, was going to betray him*' (John 6:70-71). Then, in the upper room, Jesus said to the twelve: '*You are clean, but not every one of you,*' and again, John explains that He said this: '*For he knew who was to betray him; that was why he said, "Not all of you are clean"*' (John 13:10-11).

The distinction between Judas and the other disciples is most clear in the prayer of Jesus for His disciples, where he said to the Father: '*While I was with them, I kept them in your name, which you have given me. I have guarded them, and not one of them has been lost except the son of destruction, that the Scripture might be fulfilled*' (John 17:12).

Christ 'kept' and 'guarded' the disciples, whom He describes as having been 'given' to Him by the Father. But our Lord distinguishes Judas from the other disciples. While they were kept, guarded, and given, Judas, according to the word of Jesus, was 'lost'.

Q4: Is there any hope for a person who took his or her own life?

There might be. The answer to this question is complicated by the fact that the last act of a person who takes his own life, as Judas did, was a sin. The giving and taking of life belongs to God, and taking one's own life is an act of treachery that defies God by taking into our own hands what belongs to Him.

But people enter heaven, not because they are without sin, but because their sins are covered by the blood of Jesus Christ, with whom they are united as one through the bond of faith. So, the ultimate question is always: 'Did the person who died belong to Jesus Christ?'

Responding to the widespread belief that people who take their own lives are thereby lost, Martin Luther said: 'I don't share the opinion that suicides are certainly to be damned. My reason is that they do not wish to kill themselves but are overcome by the power of the devil. They are like a man who is murdered in the woods by a robber.'[1]

The analogy of being assaulted in the woods is helpful. People suffering from mental illness or other dire circumstances may find themselves so overwhelmed by darkness that they think and act in ways that they would not normally contemplate.

In these circumstances, Paul's counsel to Timothy is especially helpful: *God's firm foundation stands, bearing this seal: 'The Lord knows those who are his,' and, 'Let everyone who names the name of the Lord depart from iniquity'* (2 Tim. 2:19).

---

1. *Luther's Works*, vol. 54, Table Talk, p. 29.

God knows who belongs to Him, and that allows us to leave the future of our loved ones in His hands. At the same time, the evidence that a person belongs to the Lord is that they turn from sin. Knowing this should act as a restraint to anyone who contemplates taking their own life.

Q5: What about eternal security?

Our Lord said of His sheep: '*They will never perish, and no one will snatch them out of my hand*' (John 10:28). But the sheep of whom He said this are those who hear His voice and follow Him (John 10:27).

Christ's sheep are the ones who follow Him. Those who do not follow Christ are not His sheep. So, although Judas followed Jesus and was involved in ministry for a time, we have to conclude from his continued defection that he was not among the people to whom Christ's great promise of security is given.

The sad fact that some people turn back from a faith they once professed should not surprise us, because the Scriptures lead us to expect it. In the parable of the sower, the seed that sprang up quickly (but was choked) and the seed in shallow ground (that was scorched) both point to professions of faith that do not last (Mark 4:5-7, 16-19).

The Gospels give us specific examples of temporary professions of faith. John tells us that many in Jerusalem believed in Jesus' name when they saw the signs that He was doing. But Jesus, for His part, '*did not entrust himself to them*' (John 2:23-24). Later, John tells us that '*many of his disciples turned back and no longer walked with him*' (John 6:66).

Taking up this theme, the book of Hebrews makes clear that it is possible for a person to know the truth, to enjoy great blessing, and even to serve fruitfully in ministry and then to abandon the faith they once professed (Heb. 6:4-6).

The apostle John gets to the heart of this issue when he speaks of those who *'went out from us because they were not of us,'* and then adds, *'if they had been of us, they would have continued with us'* (1 John 2:19).

The evidence that a person truly belongs to Christ is that they persevere. Though, like Peter, they fail in many ways, their sins and follies lead them back to Christ in the end, knowing that they are His and that He will never let them go. This perseverance is the sure evidence of saving faith.

Acknowledgments

Working on this book has been a mixed experience. Having attempted to get inside the mind of Judas, there were times when the sadness of his choices felt overwhelming to me. This sorrow only intensified my desire to see people who are walking away from Christ turn back to Him.

The joy of writing this book came from collaborating with many friends and colleagues. I am again especially indebted to John Aiello and Tim Augustyn who gave helpful input on the manuscript. I am grateful to my assistant, Sandy Williams, who transcribed a series of sermons I had preached on Judas, and to my friend Bev Savage, who gave help and inspiration with the title.

It has been a joy to work, again, with Andrew Wolgemuth, whose wise counsel has guided this project, and Rebecca Rine, whose outstanding skills as an editor made many improvements to this book.

Thanks also to William and Carine Mackenzie, and to Willie and Kate Mackenzie for their faithfulness and friendship, and to all the team at Christian Focus, including Sarah Hulley, Rosanna Burton, Paul Tollett, Alex MacAskill and Daniel van Straaten. It is a privilege to serve the Lord with you.

Heartfelt thanks to my wife Karen, whose patience, kindness and constant encouragement are a priceless gift to me.

Finally, thanks to you for reading this book. May it draw you nearer to Christ, knowing that those who seek Him are always met with mercy and grace.

Index of Scripture Sources

p.15 Abraham told Isaac that God would provide a lamb (Genesis 22:8).

p.15 God said, 'When I see the blood, I will pass over you' (Exodus 12:13).

p.15 John said, 'This is he who baptizes with the Holy Spirit' (John 1:33).

p.15 'And it shall come to pass afterwards, that I will pour out my Spirit on all flesh; your sons and your daughters shall prophesy, your old men shall dream dreams, and your young men shall see visions. Even on the male and female servants in those days I will pour out my Spirit' (Joel 2:28-29).

p.16 John 1:35, 37 refers to two of John's disciples: 'The next day again John was standing with two of his disciples... the two disciples heard him say this, and they followed Jesus.' In John 1:40, Andrew is identified as one of them: 'One of the two who heard John speak and followed Jesus was Andrew, Simon Peter's brother.'

p.16 Andrew became a disciple through the ministry of John the Baptist (John 1:35-42).

p.16 '[Andrew] brought him to Jesus. Jesus looked at him and said, "You are Simon the son of John. You shall be called Cephas" (which means Peter)' (John 1:42).

p.16 'The next day Jesus decided to go to Galilee. He found Philip and said to him, "Follow me"' (John 1:43).

p.17 'The kingdom of God is at hand; repent and believe in the gospel' (Mark 1:15).

p.17 'I know who you are— the Holy One of God' (Mark 1:24).

p.18 Jesus heals people at Peter's house (see Mark 1:29-34).

p.18 A crowd is waiting for Jesus, but he never shows up (see Mark 1:35-39).

p.20 Jesus said, 'Son, your sins are forgiven' (Mark 2:5).

p.20 Jesus said, 'Rise, pick up your bed, and go home' (Mark 2:11).

p.20 'A great crowd followed... from around Tyre and Sidon' (Mark 3:7-8).

p.21 'He appointed twelve... so that they might be with him and he might send them out to preach and have authority to cast out demons' (Mark 3:14-15).

p.22 The calling of the twelve disciples (see Luke 6:12-16).

p.23 For various names of the other Judas (see Matthew 10:3, Mark 3:18, Luke 6:16).

Chapter 2

p.25 'Judas (not Iscariot) said to him...' (John 14:22).

Chapter 3

to inherit eternal life?'
(Luke 18:18).

p.37 Jesus said, 'You lack one
thing...' (Mark 10:21).

p.38 'Disheartened by the saying,
he went away sorrowful...'
(Mark 10:22).

p.38 Jesus said, 'How difficult it is
for those who have wealth to
enter the kingdom of God!'
(Luke 18:24).

p.38 Jesus said, 'It is easier for a
camel to go through the eye
of a needle than for a rich
person to enter the kingdom
of God' (Luke 18:25).

p.38 'They were exceedingly
astonished' (Mark 10:26).

p.38 Jesus said, 'With man it is
impossible, but not with God.
For all things are possible
with God' (Mark 10:27).

p.39 'You shall have no other gods
before me' (Exodus 20:3).

p.40 Jesus said, 'No one can serve
two masters, for either he
will hate the one and love the
other, or he will be devoted
to the one and despise the
other. You cannot serve God
and money' (Matthew 6:24).

p.40 'There was a man named
Zacchaeus. He was a chief tax
collector...' (Luke 19:2).

p.40 Jesus said, 'Zacchaeus, hurry
and come down, for I must
stay at your house today'
(Luke 19:5).

p.42 Jesus said, 'Today salvation
has come to this house...'
(Luke 19:9).

p.42 'Perceiving then that they
were about to come and take
him by force to make him
king, Jesus withdrew again
to the mountain by himself'
(John 6:15).

p.43 Jesus said, 'I am the bread
of life; whoever comes to
me shall not hunger, and
whoever believes in me shall
never thirst' (John 6:35).

p.43 Jesus said, 'No one can come
to me unless the Father
who sent me draws him'
(John 6:44).

p.43 Jesus said, 'Whoever feeds
on my flesh and drinks my
blood has eternal life, and
I will raise him up on the last
day. For my flesh is true food,
and my blood is true drink'
(John 6:54, 55).

p.43 Jesus said, 'Do you take
offense at this?' (John 6:61).

p.44 Jesus said, 'There are some
of you who do not believe'
(John 6:64).

p.44 'After this many of his
disciples turned back and
no longer walked with him'
(John 6:66).

p.44 'So Jesus said to the twelve,
"Do you want to go away as
well?"' (John 6:67).

p.44 'Simon Peter answered him,
'Lord, to whom shall we go?

already been in the tomb four days' (John 11:17).

p.50 'Lord, if you had been here, my brother would not have died' (John 11:21).

p.50 'Jesus said to her, "Your brother will rise again"' (John 11:23).

p.50 'Jesus said to her, "I am the resurrection and the life. Whoever believes in me, though he die, yet shall he live"' (John 11:25).

p.50 'Then Jesus, deeply moved again, came to the tomb. It was a cave, and a stone lay against it' (John 11:38).

p.51 '[Jesus] cried out in a loud voice, "Lazarus, come out"' (John 11:43).

p.52 'A woman came up to [Jesus] with an alabaster flask of very expensive ointment, and she poured it on his head as he reclined at table' (Matthew 26:7).

p.52 'Mary therefore took a pound of expensive ointment made from pure nard, and anointed the feet of Jesus and wiped his feet with her hair' (John 12:3).

p.52 'And they scolded her' (Mark 14:5).

p.53 'There were some who said to themselves indignantly, "Why was the ointment wasted like that?"' (Mark 14:4).

p.53 'Why was this ointment not sold for three hundred denarii and given to the poor?' (John 12:5).

p.54 'He said this, not because he cared about the poor, but because he was a thief, and having charge of the moneybag he used to help himself to what was put into it' (John 12:6).

p.54 Jesus said, 'Leave her alone. Why do you trouble her? She has done a beautiful thing to me. For you always have the poor with you, and whenever you want, you can do good for them. But you will not always have me' (Mark 14:6-7).

p.54 Jesus said, 'She has anointed my body beforehand for burial' (Mark 14:8).

p.55 Jesus said, 'For even the Son of Man came not to be served but to serve, and to give his life as a ransom for many' (Mark 10:45).

p.55 Jesus said, 'If anyone would come after me, let him deny himself and take up his cross and follow me' (Mark 8:34).

p.57 'From that day on they made plans to put him to death' (John 11:53).

p.57 'Now the chief priests and the Pharisees had given orders that if anyone knew where he was, he should let them

answered him, "If I do not wash you, you have no share with me"' (John 13:8).

p.66 'Simon Peter said to him, "Lord, not my feet only but also my hands and my head!"' (John 13:9).

p.67 Jesus said, 'You are clean, but not every one of you' (John 13:10). The 'you' is plural, referring to the group (with the exception of Judas).

p.67 Jesus said, 'Truly, truly, I say to you, one of you will betray me' (John 13:21).

p.68 Jesus said, 'Did I not choose you, the twelve? And yet one of you is a devil' (John 6:70).

p.68 'He rebuked Peter and said, "Get behind me, Satan!"' (Mark 8:33).

p.68 'They were very sorrowful and began to say to him one after another, "Is it I, Lord?"' (Matthew 26:22).

p.69 The Son of Man goes as it is written of him, but woe to that man by whom the Son of Man is betrayed! (Matthew 26:24)

p.69 'Judas, who would betray him, answered, "Is it I, Rabbi?"' (Matthew 26:25).

p.69 Jesus said, 'You have said so' (Matthew 26:25).

p.70 'Simon Peter motioned to him to ask Jesus of whom he was speaking' (John 13:24).

p.70 'And they said, "Look, Lord, here are two swords"' (Luke 22:38). Peter drew his sword later that evening and cut off the ear of Malchus.

p.70 'So that disciple, leaning back against Jesus, said to him, "Lord, who is it?"' (John 13:25).

p.70 Jesus said, 'It is he to whom I will give this morsel of bread when I have dipped it' (John 13:26). William Temple suggests that no one else heard the words of Jesus to John. William Temple, *Readings in St. John's Gospel,* (Macmillan, London, 1959), p.217.

p.71 'After he had taken the morsel, Satan entered into him' (John 13:27). The evil one had also entered into Judas earlier, when he conferred with the chief priests (Luke 22:3). Satan hides himself. He is the master of disguise. Judas may not have recognized the work of Satan in him, but he would have felt its effect in the hardening of his resolve.

p.72 Jesus said, 'What you are going to do, do quickly' (John 13:27).

p.72 'Some thought that, because Judas had the moneybag, Jesus was telling him, "Buy what we need for the feast"' (John 13:29).

p.80 Jesus said, 'Judas, would you betray the Son of Man with a kiss?' (Luke 22:48).

p.80 'The kings of the earth set themselves, and the rulers take counsel together, against the Lord and against his Anointed... He who sits in the heavens laughs' (Psalm 2:2, 4).

p.80 'Kiss the Son, lest he be angry' (Psalm 2:12).

p.81 'And when those who were around him saw what would follow, they said, "Lord, shall we strike with the sword?"' (Luke 22:49). Peter's question suggests that the guards had drawn their swords already, as they would have done if about to make the arrest.

p.81 'No more of this!' Luke 22:51.

p.82 Jesus said, 'Put your sword back into its place. For all who take the sword will perish by the sword' (Matthew 26:52).

p.82 Jesus said, 'Do you think that I cannot appeal to my Father, and he will at once send me more than twelve legions of angels?' (Matthew 26:53).

p.82 Jesus said, 'Shall I not drink the cup that the Father has given me?' (John 18:11).

p.82 'No one takes it [my life] from me, but I lay it down of my own accord. I have authority to lay it down and I have authority to take it up again' (John 10:18).

p.83 'And one of them struck the servant of the high priest and cut off his right ear... and [Jesus] touched his ear and healed him' (Luke 22:50, 51).

p.83 'Judas came, one of the twelve, and with him a great crowd with swords and clubs, from the chief priests and the elders of the people' (Matthew 26:47). 'Judas, having procured... some officers from the chief priests and Pharisees' (John 18:3).

p.83 Jesus said, 'Have you come out as against a robber, with swords and clubs to capture me? Day after day I was with you in the temple teaching, and you did not seize me. But let the Scriptures be fulfilled' (Mark 14:48-49).

p.83 'And they all left him and fled' (Mark 14:50).

p.83 'So the band of soldiers and their captain and the officers of the Jews arrested Jesus and bound him' (John 18:12).

p.83 'No one could bind him anymore, not even with a chain' (Mark 5:3).

Chapter 7

p.86 Jesus said, 'Whoever is ashamed of me and of my words...of him will the Son

deserving death has been done by him' (Luke 23:15).

p.91 'Now the chief priests and the elders persuaded the crowd to ask for Barabbas and destroy Jesus' (Matthew 27:20).

p.91 Pilate said, 'Then what shall I do with Jesus who is called Christ?' (Matthew 27:21).

p.91 'They all said, "Let him be crucified!"' (Matthew 27:22).

p.91 Pilate said, 'Why? What evil has he done?' (Matthew 27:23).

p.91 'So when Pilate saw that he was gaining nothing, but rather that a riot was beginning, he took water and washed his hands before the crowd, saying, "I am innocent of this man's blood; see to it yourselves"' (Matthew 27:24).

p.91 Pilate said, 'I have found in him no guilt deserving death. I will therefore punish and release him' (Luke 23:22).

p.92 Pilate said, 'See, I am bringing him out to you that you may know that I find no guilt in him' (John 19:4).

p.92 'So Jesus came out, wearing the crown of thorns and the purple robe' (John 19:5).

p.92 'From then on Pilate sought to release him' (John 19:12).

p.92 'If you release this man, you are not Caesar's friend' (John 19:12).

p.93 '[Pilate] released the man who had been thrown into prison for insurrection and murder' (Luke 23:25).

p.93 'So when Pilate heard these words, he brought Jesus out and sat down on the judgment seat at a place called The Stone Pavement' (John 19:13).

p.93 'It was about the sixth hour' (John 19:14). We know from Mark 15:25 that our Lord was crucified at the third hour (9 a.m.). Bishop Westcott suggests that John's reference to the sixth hour was in reference to Roman time counted from midnight— hence 6 a.m., and that Mark's reference to the third hour counted time from sunrise, hence 9 a.m.

p.93 'When Judas, his betrayer, saw that Jesus was condemned, he changed his mind and brought back the thirty pieces of silver' (Matthew 27:3).

p.94 'It was the third hour when they crucified him' (Mark 15:25).

p.95 Judas said, 'I have sinned by betraying innocent blood' (Matthew 27:4).

p.95 'They said, "What is that to us?"' (Matthew 27:4).

p.96 'And throwing down the pieces of silver into the temple, [Judas] departed' (Matthew 27:5).

Christian Focus Publications

Our mission statement –

STAYING FAITHFUL
In dependence upon God we seek to impact the world through literature faithful to His infallible Word, the Bible. Our aim is to ensure that the Lord Jesus Christ is presented as the only hope to obtain forgiveness of sin, live a useful life and look forward to heaven with Him.

Our books are published in four imprints:

CHRISTIAN
FOCUS

Popular works including biographies, commentaries, basic doctrine and Christian living.

CHRISTIAN
HERITAGE

Books representing some of the best material from the rich heritage of the church.

MENTOR

Books written at a level suitable for Bible College and seminary students, pastors, and other serious readers. The imprint includes commentaries, doctrinal studies, examination of current issues and church history.

CF4•K

Children's books for quality Bible teaching and for all age groups: Sunday school curriculum, puzzle and activity books; personal and family devotional titles, biographies and inspirational stories – because you are never too young to know Jesus!

Christian Focus Publications Ltd,
Geanies House, Fearn, Ross-shire,
IV20 1TW, Scotland, United Kingdom.
www.christianfocus.com
blog.christianfocus.com